Joseph Townsend

A Journey Through Spain in the Years 1786 and 1787

Joseph Townsend

A Journey Through Spain in the Years 1786 and 1787

ISBN/EAN: 9783744753500

Printed in Europe, USA, Canada, Australia, Japan

Cover: Foto ©Andreas Hilbeck / pixelio.de

More available books at **www.hansebooks.com**

A

JOURNEY

THROUGH

SPAIN

IN THE YEARS 1786 AND 1787;

WITH PARTICULAR ATTENTION

TO THE

AGRICULTURE, MANUFACTURES, COMMERCE,
POPULATION, TAXES, AND REVENUE

OF THAT COUNTRY;

AND

REMARKS

IN PASSING THROUGH

A PART OF FRANCE.

―――

By JOSEPH TOWNSEND, A.M.
RECTOR OF PEWSEY, WILTS;
AND LATE OF CLARE-HALL, CAMBRIDGE.

―――

IN THREE VOLUMES.——VOL. III.

―――

LONDON:
PRINTED FOR C. DILLY, IN THE POULTRY.
M.DCC.XCI.

ERRATA.

Page line.
19. 16. *for* Ciudador, *lege* Ciudad, or.
21. 17. O man, *lege* O mal.
79. 5.   hijos de dalgo, *lege* hijos dalgo.
316. 16. *dele* more so.

CONTENTS
OF
VOL. III.

	Page
VOYAGE from Cadiz to Malaga, with Obfervations on the Influx into the Mediterranean, and Sea Breezes —	1
Malaga, with an Account of its Wines —	10
The Environs of Malaga — —	35
Journey from Malaga to Granada, with general Obfervations on the Ploughs of Spain — — —	43
Granada, with an Account of the Alhambra, Silk Manufacture, the Expulfion of the Moors, and Conjectures refpecting the Formation of Nitre - —	55
Journey from Granada to Carthagena, with Obfervations on Poverty and Poor Laws	96
Carthagena, with the Dock-Yard, Galley Slaves, the Fifheries, Manufacture of Efparto Rufh, Barilla, Commerce, Difeafes, Manners, &c. — —	121
Journey, from Carthagena, through Murcia, to Alicant — —	149
Alicant, its Commerce and Improvements	163

Alicant

CONTENTS.

	Page
Alicant, its Workhouse and Citadel	184
Environs of Alicant, with the Huerta and Pantano	191
Barilla, and its corresponding Species	198
Granakermes, and its Natural History	202
Locusts, and their History	206
Weights and Measures of Alicant	223
Journey from Alicant to Valencia	225
Valencia, its Situation, Buildings, Pictures, University, Workhouse, Monte Pio, Manufactures of Silk, Tiles, &c. Commerce, Agriculture, Amusements, Customs, &c.	235
Journey from Valencia to Barcelona through Morviedro, Benicarlo, Tortosa, and Tarragona	290
Return to Barcelona, with Observations on the Population, Taxes, and Revenue of Catalonia, an Account of the Inquisition, and special Remarks on the Causes of the Prosperity of that Province	319
The Inquisition at Barcelona	333
Physicians at Barcelona	340
Instructions and Inquiries of Philip II. to gain a Knowledge of his Kingdom	348

VOYAGE

FROM

CADIZ TO MALAGA.

ON Friday, 23d of March, at eight in the morning, I went on board a little brig, which came from Yarmouth, and was bound for Malaga; but as it was an hour too late for the tide when we got under way, we had the mortification to see other vessels make good their passage, whilst we, after beating about the bay six hours, were reduced to the necessity of coming to an anchor. For my consolation, I had thus an opportunity of dining once more with my amiable friend count de Greppi, and of lodging again under the hospitable roof of Mr. Duff.

Early the next morning we set sail with a pleasant breeze, and before night, entering the straits of Gibraltar, had the satisfaction to view the proud rock, at the sight of which every British heart should triumph in the recollection, not so much of the courage of its brave defender, as of his generous compassion for his besiegers in the hour of their distress. As we had the advantage of the current, we slackened sail, that we might be certain of not passing Malaga before the morning. But, by the time that we had entered the bay, and began to see the city at a distance, the wind died away, and for two hours we found ourselves becalmed. However, as the day advanced, the sea breeze got up, and soon carried us to the place of our destination.

We have here two phenomena, universally noticed, but never sufficiently accounted for: the constant influx into the Mediterranean, and the sea breeze. Both have occupied the attention of philosophers; and their solutions, however satisfactory to themselves, have not, as I conceive, removed the difficulties involved in these subjects.

Doctor Halley, in his experiments to ascertain the quantity evaporated from the Mediterranean Sea, placing a vessel of saltwater over burning coals, brought it to the temperament of the air in our hottest summer; and at the end of two hours, having found the evaporation and the proportion of the surfaces to each other, from these he formed his calculation. He then attempted to discover the quantity of water annually poured into the Mediterranean by all its rivers, making his calculation by the produce of the Thames; and finding this unequal to the evaporation, he concluded, that he had assigned a sufficient cause for the constant influx. How inaccurate the premises! how hasty the conclusion! Not to mention his comparing the discharge from rapid streams, borne with impetuosity into the Mediterranean, and retaining their freshness at the distance of many leagues from shore, with the more humble produce of the Thames, creeping almost imperceptibly along, and lost as soon as it has reached the sea; not to mention the impropriety of this comparison, it may be sufficient to remark, that the whole quantity of water contained in his veffel was brought to the temperature of the air in our hotteft fummer. No wonder then, that he fhould make the evaporation from the furface of the Mediterranean amount to two hundred and eighty millions of tons per day. But that furface is feldom, and but for very tranfient moments, of the fame degree of heat with the incumbent atmofphere, becaufe every breeze muft make a confiderable variation in its temperature, by commixing the waters from a confiderable depth with thofe that are fuperficial. In a moft interefting voyage among the Alps, by M. de Sauffure, we find fome experiments conducted by himfelf on the lake of Geneva, by which it appears, that on the 6th of Auguft, 1774, the thermometer of Reaumur at the depth of three hundred and twelve feet, ftood at eight degrees and an half, when near the furface it was fifteen degrees, and, in the air, twenty degrees.

Here we find five degrees of difference between the heat of the atmofphere and the furface of the water in calm weather; but how much greater would have been the variation, had the lake been ruffled by a storm,

storm, more especially had the waters been troubled to the depth of six hundred and twenty feet, where, as it seems, the thermometer sunk down to four degrees three-twentieths.

Hence it appears, that the calculations of Dr. Halley are ill grounded. That his conclusion is erroneous, will be evident, if we reflect, that supposing the evaporation to exceed the annual supply from rivers, the Mediterranean Sea would be constantly growing more briny than the ocean, till, in process of time, it would become one solid mass of salt.

This being the case, some other cause must be assigned for this interesting phenomenon. Supposing the fact to be well established, that the influx at the straits of Gibraltar does really exist, without any corresponding efflux by the same channel, there must be some invisible communication between the Mediterranean and the ocean; and this, considering the strong convulsion our globe has at some period suffered, is by no means improbable.

The other phenomenon, not sufficiently accounted for, is the sea breeze. It has been supposed to arise merely from the accumulation of heat on the earth by day; as the land breeze is conceived to originate from the diminution of that heat by night. But we might enquire, whether the surface of the earth, by night, becomes colder than the surface of the water? if not, should not the sea breeze continue all the night? but this would be contrary to fact. That accurate observer, Dampier, has given a good description of these alternate changes in the direction of the wind on the coast, and at a few leagues distance from the land. He says, " The sea breeze begins about nine " in the morning, so gently, as if it were " afraid to approach the shore; and then, " as if unwilling to offend, it makes a halt, " and seems ready to retire. It increases " till noon, and dies away about five in the " evening."

From the result of some experiments confirmed by my own observation, I am induced to believe that the sea breeze originates in the ascent of vapour from the sea, and the land breeze from the condensation of that vapour.

That one cubic foot of water may be

converted into sixteen thousand feet of steam, in the medium pressure of our atmosphere, we learn from Mr. Watt; and although vapour formed by the sun is not so rare as steam arising from the surface of boiling water, yet we know that the space it occupies, and the force of its expansion, are considerable. To ascertain this matter, I took a twelve ounce phial, half filled with water, in which I placed a tube, two feet long, and nearly one-quarter of an inch diameter in its bore. This tube I cemented so perfectly, that no air could pass between it and the mouth of the phial. Thus prepared, I exposed my apparatus to the sun, when instantly a vapour began to form, of a force sufficient to overcome the pressure of the atmosphere, and by degrees to make the water rise up four-and-twenty inches in my tube. But whilst even the thinnest cloud was passing before the sun, the water sunk in the tube with great rapidity, rising again slowly after the gleam returned. At sun-set, when the whole of the vapour was condensed, and a dew collected on the internal surface of the phial, the water sunk down

down again till it had found its level. At the clofing of the day, the dew collected on that fide of the phial which was turned from the fun; but in the night it was again taken up, and the whole before the morning was depofited on the other fide neareft to the window, being always condenfed on the fide which was relatively cold.

How often do we obferve the fun diffipating a thick fog, and converting it into that fpecies of vapour, which, when the thermometer is above fifty-five degrees, is invifible. M. de Sauffure remarked upon Col Ferret, a mountain of the Alps, bounding the Allée blanche, one thoufand one hundred and ninety-five toifes, or about feven thoufand feet above the level of the fea, that whenever the fun fhone ftrongly upon the valley, it diffolved the clouds as foon as they entered it. But this never happened oppofite the glaciers; for there, as if attracted by the ice, they defcended rapidly, and feemed to fpread themfelves upon it. § 865.

From fome of the higheft rocks he often
faw

faw the vapours, after fun-fet, gradually depreffed, and concentrating themfelves in the bottom of the vallies. § 1126.

Agreeable to thefe remarks mariners obferve, that wind is generated by a fingle cloud.

During the time, therefore, that vapour is produced, the wind blows from the fea; but whilft the condenfation lafts, it comes off the land.

We availed ourfelves of a gentle fea breeze; and, traverfing the bay, we came into the harbour.

MALAGA.

MALAGA.

IN sailing up the Mediterranean, when first you open Malaga, you see it deeply embayed, and on the land side surrounded by high and rugged mountains, which seem to be destitute of soil, and, therefore, not susceptible of cultivation; but, as you approach, the prospect every way improves, the vineyards are distinctly seen on the declivities, hanging towards the sun, and all the lower lands appear to be exceedingly productive.

As soon as we had dropt our anchor, an officer appeared, to whom I communicated my desire of going immediately on shore, to deliver a letter to the marquis of Vallehermoso, captain-general of the province.

Having

Having looked at the direction, after due examination respecting health, he gave us Prattique, to the no small satisfaction of our master, who feared that we might have been obliged to wait for it two days, as often happens, arising either from the perverseness or neglect of the officer on duty.

Malaga is situated in a valley of no great extent, on the side of a deep ravin, which in summer contains no water, but in winter affords a bed to a considerable river. The houses are high; the streets are contracted, many of them not more than eight feet wide, others not so wide; all badly paved, and dirty to a proverb. It is divided into six parishes, and contains forty-one thousand five hundred and ninety-two souls; of which by far the greatest proportion is of females; because, of those who arrive at the age of maturity, and go out to labour, here are found six women to one man. They have twenty-five convents; fifteen for monks, and ten for nuns; with nine hospitals, and one beaterio.

Of the buildings, whether public or private, the only one, in the least worthy of attention, is the cathedral, an edifice begun
A. D.

A. D. 1528, and not yet finished. It is indeed two hundred years since it was so far brought to a conclusion as to be fitted for the performance of divine service; but notwithstanding new taxes are granted for its completion, and have been collected for near seventy years, it remains with one single tower out of six contained in the original design. The dimensions are three hundred and sixty feet by one hundred and eighty, with one hundred and thirty-five in height. It is a noble pile; but the part which most rivets the attention, is the choir, admirable for the perfection of its carved works, representing in very bold relief the twelve apostles and the most distinguished of the saints.

This bishopric is worth a hundred and fifty thousand ducats, or £.16,479. 9s. 10d. But then, one-third of this revenue is disposed of by the king. The whole chapter consists of the bishop, with eight dignitaries, twelve canons, twelve minor canons, and the same number of prebendaries. Of the former, the dean receives six hundred pounds a year; but the other dignitaries only four hundred and fifty pounds.

The

The convents, though numerous, are few of them remarkable, either for architecture, or for any monuments of art. Of the friars, the Franciscans seem to take the lead, and to be most the objects of veneration among the common people; of these, they have four orders, but I am not acquainted with their distinctive characters. A gentleman, who is no friend to the monastic institutions, was so obliging as to give me the subsequent description, but this relates only to externals:

> Barb sans poux, et poux sans barb:
> Barb et poux: ni poux ni barb.

Among these, the Capuchins appear to be the only useful members of society, giving themselves up to the service of the poor; yet even they might be dispensed with, and their place supplied with more advantage to the public, by the fathers of the oratory, or congregation of S. Philip Neri; who, although not bound by vows, are more laborious and more extensively useful, than all the regulars of the monastic tribes.

As one of my friends was retired, with other young people, to this congregation for a few days, to be engaged in reading, prayer, and meditation, previous to their receiving the eucharist at Easter; I went to visit him in his retreat, and was much pleased with the attention paid by the fathers in preparing their minds for this solemnity.

In the evening I returned to hear the penitential sermon and the miserere; when, as usual, the lights were extinguished, and the flagellation, accompanied by the miserere, was begun; it became evident, by the fervor of their devotion and the vehemence of their discipline, more than commonly protracted, that the penitents, either deeply impressed with a sense of guilt, were more than commonly solicitous to placate an offended deity; or that, mistaking his nature, they earnestly desired to please him by their voluntary sufferings. It is much to be lamented, that the fathers of the oratory, so highly to be respected for their good intentions, should not hold up the idea of reformation to their penitents, rather than flat-

ter

ter and deceive them with the vain hope of thus making an atonement for their crimes.

These fathers use the discipline on Wednesdays and Fridays, about seven in the evening, because at that time, immediately after the vespers, they rehearse their mattins; but all the religious orders, who rise at midnight to this service, perform their flagellation in its proper season; and many of them do it with such violence, that in the morning, the places where they stood, are found sprinkled with their blood. The bishop of Malaga, although distinguished for his benevolence and piety, and, in the opinion of mankind, free from every stain, yet is said to practise secret discipline with more severity than the most zealous of the monks.

This good bishop, not satisfied with giving thus his body to the scourge, gives more than half his goods to feed the poor, who assemble every morning at his doors, to receive each a little bit of money, and from thence disperse themselves among the convents, where they never fail to get some bread and broth.

Beside these general benefactors, many of the merchants are exceedingly liberal in their donations to the poor; and among them, no one is more distinguished than D. Joseph Martinis, a gentleman equally celebrated for the extent of his information, the hospitality of his table, and the bountiful assistance which he never fails to give to objects of distress. The poor are at all times welcome to his doors, where money is daily distributed, and for them every day his caldron boils. His most intimate friend assured me, that, with his own hands, he gave them more than eight hundred pounds a year. About eleven in the morning they begin to swarm about his habitation, young and old, the feeble and the robust, men, women, and children, clothed in rags, and half devoured by vermin; where, seated on the ground, they employ themselves in the most disgusting occupation, till the hour for distributing the meat and broth arrives; after which, they either lie down to sleep, or disperse themselves about the streets to beg, varying, as it may be readily conceived,

ceived, their plan, according to the variation of the season.

With such encouragement for beggars, no wonder that they should abound in Malaga, where the lazy can have no inducement to employ themselves in labour, and where the profligate, when they shall have wasted their substance, may know for a certainty that they shall never be in want of bread. Hence it comes to pass, that in the city, few traces of industry are seen, whilst filth and nastiness, immorality and vice, wretchedness and poverty, the inevitable consequences of undistinguishing benevolence, prevail. How evident is it from hence, that he, who finds employment for the poor, is their greatest friend; whilst he, who indiscriminately feeds them, should be ranked among their enemies.

Multitudes of beggars, infesting every street, mark a bad police; and certainly few cities have more cause than Malaga to complain of this. For some time I could not conceive the reason, why, wherever I had supped, I was constantly attended to my lodging by a servant with a light; but observing upon some occasion, that such attendance would be **needlefs**, becaufe the ftars fhone bright, and the diftance was inconfiderable; I was informed, that the fervant and the light were not merely for comfort, but for fafety, becaufe robberies and murders were frequent in the night. Indeed when I was there, an officer, returning unattended to his lodging, was affaulted in the ftreet by thieves, and, upon making **refiftance**, was ftabbed in the back by one, whilft another robbed him. In the laft fixteen months they reckoned feventy murders; for which, not one criminal had been brought to juftice; and in one year, as I am credibly informed, a hundred and five perfons fell in the fame manner. Similar to this had been the confequence of grofs neglect and miftaken lenity at Cadiz, till count O'Reilley became its governor. Whenever fuch a man fhall be named to the government of Malaga, the fame Herculean labour will be undertaken here, and probably with the fame good effect.

Their form of municipal government is excellent, but the defect is in its mal-adminiftration.

At the head of this department ftands

the

the governor, representing majesty, and himself, when absent, represented by the *corregidor* with his *alcalde mayor*, the former resembling the mayor of our corporations, the latter performing the office of recorder. Both these are in the nomination of the crown. The alcalde goes his rounds in the beginning of the night, attended by an *escrivano*.

Of the *regidores*, or aldermen, two in rotation preside monthly. These have the privilege of selling their places, or of naming a successor; but should they neglect, whilst living, to dispose of their office, it goes by succession to the heir, either son or brother, being *hijos de la ciudador*, free citizens. Should they have purchased, they may easily contrive to reimburse themselves.

The *alcaldes de barrio*, or petty constables, are twelve, of which six are named by the regidores, the other six are chosen by the people. They have staves, and walk the streets, two hours each, every night. They have the power to arrest till morning, and may command the assistance of the military.

The *alguazil mayor*, chosen by the regidores from among themselves, like our constable of the hundred, is endued with more extensive authority than the alcaldes de barrio; having the power of arrest over a whole district, yet subject always to the alcalde mayor, and obliged to give him an account of every thing he has done.

The *escrivanos*, or public notaries and scriveners, are twenty-four, to examine witnesses, and make minutes. No deposition can be taken but by them, nor any judgment pronounced but on their report.

The *syndicos* are two, chosen annually by the people, to watch both for them and for the king, that neither they may be oppressed, nor the revenue be defrauded. Of these, one is subjected to the approbation of the crown, whilst his associate is altogether independent of the court. This officer, called *personero del comun*, is by the patent of creation, dated 5th May, 1766, like a Roman tribune, armed with his *veto* in the assembly of the regidores, among whom he sits, and may communicate at all times with the king, either in person, when it suits him to demand an audience, or by letter. Without his consent, the regidores cannot regulate the price of provisions, and, when regulated, he inspects the quality.

The present alcalde mayor, little respected for his personal appearance, less admired for the endowments of his mind, and not proof himself against corruption, seems to have neither inclination nor abilities to curb the rapacity of the *escrivanos* or notaries, who, taking bribes to the right and to the left, prevent justice, by drawing up false reports; always prepared to skreen for money the vilest offenders. Hence the adage,

O bien; O man; tienta al escribano.

Murders and assassinations, with every species of excess and violence, must, without the strenuous exertions of the magistrate and the strict execution of the laws, be frequent in a country, where, whenever the wind blows over land, all the passions are inflamed, in some persons almost to frenzy. And yet here, justice, when most awakened, pursues offenders with a tardy step, flow in its approach, uncertain in its vengeance. Innumerable instances are cited of criminals, who have died forgotten in the prisons; and of some who, whilst under sentence of death, having married and produced a numerous offspring, have been brought forth to execution, when all recollection of their crimes had been long since obliterated. A friend of mine in Malaga informed me, that he saw a woman, after nine years confinement, hanged, for having poisoned two husbands, and one mother-in-law.

The usual pretext for this neglect, is the desire, by repeated examinations of the criminal at distant periods, and by the enquiries consequent on his confessions, to get a knowledge of his accomplices; but the misfortune is, that by this delay, the purposes of justice are defeated.

In summer the inhabitants of these sultry regions, excluding as much as possible the sun, confine themselves to their habitations throughout the day; but when the overwhelming heat is succeeded by the refreshing coolness of the evening, they wander abroad, and when the light is gone,

all

all the young people bathe for hours in the sea. The sexes, however, do not bathe promiscuously, but separate, and at a convenient distance from each other. At such seasons, to prevent intrusion, the spot where the ladies are, is guarded by sentinels with their loaded muskets; and should a gentleman be so indiscreet as to swim round to them, it must be at the hazard of his life. Whenever, therefore, a young person is determined to intrude, he goes in disguise, as the female attendant of some easy fair one, and in that character passes unobserved.

This practice of bathing every night, is not designed so much for pleasure as for health, being meant to obviate every inconvenience experienced from the heat. Yet notwithstanding all precautions, the diseases of a relaxed fibre are most prevalent; for, not to mention those which arise from irritability of nerves as the consequence of debility, tertians and putrid fevers rage with such violence, that more than three thousand died last year in the hospital of S. Juan de Dios, beside multitudes in the city and its environs.

I happened to be at Malaga in the holy week, and although the ceremonies are not equal to thofe of Barcelona, yet they are conducted with fome degree of folemnity, and afford much amufement to the vulgar.

On Thurfday morning the confecrated hoft was depofited in a maufoleum, erected for the purpofe at a great expence; and of three keys, one was tied round the bifhop's neck, who leaving fome of the canons to keep watch and ward, which they did through the night, retired himfelf to dine with thirteen poor men, after which he wafhed their feet.

In the evening they fang the miferere, accompanied by foft mufic, and with fuch expreffion that fcarcely any one, endued with fenfibility, could refrain from tears.

On Friday, by feven in the morning, nearly ten thoufand people were affembled in the great fquare to view proceffions; but juft as a crucifix was feen entering at one corner of the fquare, whilft the beloved difciple, with the bleffed Virgin, made their appearance at the other, a fudden fhower compelled the multitude to difperfe
for

for shelter. Thus unfortunately, the meeting of the son and mother was prevented; otherwise these, and a variety of images, were to have acted their several parts. John was to have expressed his sorrow by lifting up his hand, the blessed Virgin would have fainted, and all the people would have been dissolved in tears.

In the evening every one resorted to the cathedral, the sacred lights were extinguished, and the miserere was again repeated, after the host had been removed from the sepulchre to the high altar. This, to a good catholic, should be a most desireable moment, because he may gain one thousand and sixty days indulgence, every time he repeats " praised be the holy hearts " of Christ and of the Virgin."

On Saturday morning, the resurrection was announced with all the usual tokens of exulting joy, and every one prepared to keep the feast. For this purpose more than a thousand lambs had been brought into the market the preceding night, and after the example of the Israelites, every family which could afford to purchase one, was zealous to keep up the remembrance of

the

the christian passover. Light was re-kindled, and consecrated; and to represent the bright luminary of the church, a wax candle, twelve feet high, and twelve inches in diameter, pierced by five awls, was placed near the altar. Attendance on this ceremony procures for the penitent fourscore days indulgence. The value of which may be estimated, either by money or by corporal severities; because, as Mr. Gibbon, who in this case is a competent witness, informs us, four pounds for the rich, and nine shillings for the poor, or three thousand lashes, are equal to one year's penance.

In the evening I observed hundreds of lambs, decorated with coloured ribbons, led by the boys about the streets. The market for these continued the three days of Easter, during which they enter free of every duty: whereas at other seasons, although calves and lambs entering the city are discharged from the millones, there is paid for them an alcavala of four per cent. on the value.

The country round Malaga appears wild and broken. The mountains are high, rugged,

rugged, pointed, and at their summits destitute of soil, yet cultivated wherever a vine can be fixed. The rock under the broken fragments of schist is limestone and marble. The fruit trees are the algarroba, figs, almonds, vines, oranges, and lemons, with the aloes, producing here the prickly pear in such abundance, that the tithe of them is let for thirty thousand reals, or three hundred pounds a year.

The chief dependance of this country is on the vines. These are cultivated with much labour, and at a great expence; for beside the common pruning twice a year, and the collecting of the fruit, all the earth near each plant must be twice moved. Previous to the winter it is collected round the stem, that the roots may be kept dry and healthy during the wet season; and before the great heats of summer, it is formed into a dish to retain the water, that the vine may not droop for want of moisture.

When it is considered that these vineyards are always on the declivity of hills, inclined towards the scorching sun, it may be readily conceived that the labour is severe;

fevere; and that the people, who with unremitted application perform this tafk, can never deferve the character of drones. The peafants of no country upon earth are more patient of heat, of hunger, and of thirft, or capable of greater exertions, than this very people, who have been accufed of indolence. For my part, from what I have obferved, and have been able to collect, I am fatisfied, that if the Spaniards of the interior provinces are unemployed, it is to be attributed neither to the climate, nor to their conftitutions; but either to the neglects of government, or to other accidental caufes already noticed and explained.

The expence attending the cultivation of a vineyard is fo confiderable, being equal to three-quarters of the produce, that none but the lands unfit for corn are converted to this ufe, and many which formerly yielded wine in great abundance are now neglected. According to the ftatement of Oforio, who wrote towards the clofe of the laft century, three ½ gallons of wine, the produce of twice that quantity of grapes, as it came from the prefs, coft one fhilling and two-pence for the labour, being

ing the very price at which it was fold in the villages, when the grape was plentiful. Notwithstanding the diminution in the quantity of land allotted to the vine, there are, in the diftrict of Malaga, fourteen thoufand vine-preffes, chiefly employed in making the rich wines, which, if white, from the nature of the country, is called mountain; if red, from the colour, *vino tinto*, known to us by the name of tent.

For the purpofe of making thefe wines fuller in the body, and fweeter than they would naturally be, the grapes are left to be very ripe, then being cut, they are expofed to the fun to evaporate their moifture; after which, they are preffed and put into veffels, with a due proportion of infpiffated vinous fyrop. Some late experiments of M. John Murphy, prove that the mountains of Malaga can produce a light and pleafant white wine, equal in quality to the beft fherry. To obtain this, when he has gathered his fruit, he combs off the grapes from the ftem, before he commits them to the prefs. I have tafted the produce both in England, and at his table, and think it already fuperior to the fherry, commonly to be be met with, and have no doubt that he will improve it every year, till he has brought it to be equal to the best.

This wine he sells for sixteen pounds the butt, of one hundred and thirty-five gallons, delivered on board the ship; whereas sherry sells for twenty-four, and is frequently spoiled with brandy.

Good mountain is sold from thirteen to sixteen pounds the butt, according to quality and age.

It is reckoned, that from eight hundred to a thousand vessels enter this port every year, of which about one-tenth are Spanish; and the exports in wine, fruit, oil, and fish, are computed at about three hundred and seventy-five thousand pounds per annum; but there have been times when it has been considerably more. M. Martinis alone one year exported five thousand butts of wine, and other merchants in the same proportion to their usual sales. Their fish are anchovies, of which, in years of great abundance, they have sold ten thousand *baricas* of two quintals each.

In my little excursions round the city, I visited the *Victoria*, a convent built in the
valley

valley between the old Moorish fortress, and the hill on which Ferdinand erected his battery. My guide, a good old monk, endeavoured to amuse me with a legendary tale respecting this spot, and the reason of its having been thus honoured; but my attention was otherwise engaged, for I was taking notice of some people busily employed in pulling up oats from a fine crop of wheat. From their mode of winnowing their grain, after the mares have trodden it with their feet, their seed corn must be very foul; whereas, with the simple machine I have referred to, the drum and principle of which was first described by Papin, they might save the expence of pulling up the oats, and keep their land much cleaner than at present.

How wonderful is it, that this beautiful machine is not better known, and that it should not yet have been universally adopted. Dr. Papin invented it in 1689, merely for the purposes of raising water, and of supplying deep mines with air; but, in Holland, it was adapted to the use of husbandmen, for winnowing their corn. This great philosopher published his discovery to the world

world in a valuable work called *Recueil de diverses Pieces touchant quelques nouvelles Machines*, printed at Caſſel, in 1695. He called this machine *Rotatilis Suctor et Preſſor*.

I have been the more particular on this ſubject, becauſe a tallow-chandler in London has lately aſſumed the invention to himſelf and taken out a patent, although, as it thus appears, neither the machine itſelf, nor the purpoſes to which he would apply it, have any claim to novelty.

Near the convent of Victoria I took notice of ſome blue marly clay, of which are made the earthen jugs, called *bucaros* and alcarrazas, uſed in this part of Spain for cooling water. It is remarkable, that when the ſcorching *terral* wind prevails, liquids expoſed to it in theſe jugs, become as cold as if buried in the ſnow; but, if ſubjected to the influence of the eaſt wind, they ſoon grow warm. To explain this, we muſt obſerve that the *bucaros* being porous, ſuffer the water to tranſude, and to cover, as with dew, the external ſurface of the veſſel; in conſequence of which, being expoſed to the dry land wind, the evaporation is carried

ried on with rapidity, and, in proportion to the evaporation is the cold thereby produced; whilst the east wind, sweeping along the surface of the sea, becomes saturated with moisture, and therefore not only is itself incapable of carrying on the process of evaporation, and of increasing cold, but, operating as warm vapour, it has an opposite effect.

The effect of evaporation no where appears more striking than in the East Indies, where, for the purpose of procuring ice, they make large pits in wide extended plains, and nearly filling them with canes, they place on these, very shallow pans, unglazed and porous, and filled with boiling water. Thus exposed during the night to the influence of the land breeze, a pellicle of ice is formed before the morning on the surface of the water, always thicker if the wind has been warmer than usual.

When I was returned from the Victoria, the young count de Villalcazar, to whom, as well as to his father, I was under the highest obligations for their polite attentions, invited me to take a ride with him to see his country-house called the *Retiro*.

It is indeed a beautiful retreat, fituated on a declivity at the feet of the mountains, and not far diftant from the fea; both which, with Malaga, contribute to enrich its profpects. It is a very ancient habitation, in the form of a caftle; but as it was never ftrong, it muft have been defigned only to prevent furprife from the nocturnal vifits of the Moorifh pirates. The numerous fountains in the garden are pretty, and well fupplied with water. The fruit trees are luxuriant. Here oranges, lemons, limes, citrons, olives, vines, apricots, figs, and almonds, mix together in beautiful confufion. Could I have prolonged my ftay at Malaga, I fhould frequently have vifited this enchanting fpot.

This little excurfion prepared me for one to a greater diftance from the city.

Whilft I was attending the folemnities of Eafter in the cathedral, I became acquainted with a perfon who happened to ftand near to me, and who, after anfwering my enquiries, and explaining to me fuch ceremonies as moft excited my attention, had the goodnefs to invite me to his houfe. Struck with the franknefs of his manner,

I ac-

I accepted the invitation and went home with him, where I had the happiness of finding, in the person of his father, one of the most sensible and most intelligent of those, who honoured me with their friendship and esteem.

After I became more intimate in the family, this gentleman, called don Felix Solesio, pressed me to spend a few days with him at his country-seat. On the eve of my departure my time was precious; yet, such was the cordiality of his invitation, that I determined to comply with it.

On Thursday, 12th April, we left the city, and, travelling westward, in a few hours we arrived at S. Carlos, near to *Aroyo de la Miel,* in the vicinity of which the snow continued still unmelted on the mountains. Here don Felix has just finished a spacious mansion, with an extensive garden; the latter well planted with every thing the soil and climate can admit of; the former, though vast, yet inelegant, and destitute of taste. Utility being every where consulted, without the least attention to appearance, the poultry-yard and pig-sties are in the rfont of the house, and in the whole pile

there

there is not one good room, nor the least regard to symmetry, but all the apartments are scattered and void of order, as if built without a plan. At his table appears the greatest affluence, and nothing but plate is to be seen; yet the same want of symmetry prevails, and the same deficiency of refinement, as if he had previously determined to have nothing modern. His eldest son, my first acquaintance, seems here to be unemployed; whilst the second, an active youth, overlooks the labourers, and occasionally works among them.

The estate they cultivate, is more than two leagues in length, and one in breadth, by the sea side, and hanging to the sun. Much of the land is good, the rest only fit for sheep; and the whole quantity, as near as I could calculate, is about twelve thousand acres, for the fee-simple of which he gave twenty thousand hard dollars, or four thousand pounds sterling.

It is but two years since he made the purchase, and in that short space of time he has planted two hundred thousand vines, five thousand olives, one hundred and twenty thousand mulberries, five hundred and
eighty

eighty figs, three hundred pomegranates, seven hundred lemons, and as many orange trees, beside a great number of sugar canes. He has added to his works a tan-yard, and a paper-mill, each upon an extensive scale.

To conduct all these operations, he has engaged one hundred and twelve men, the labourers at five reals (one shilling) a day, the masons at nine. Last year he constantly employed between seven and eight hundred.

His present stock upon his farm consists of fifty-six oxen, twelve hundred sheep, four hundred goats, and one hundred and fifty-eight pigs; but all these will be increased.

The shepherds sleep near their flocks, and every night a watchman well armed rides round the whole estate, to see that all is safe. Were it not for this precaution, the thieves by profession, and the smugglers, when distressed, would commit frequent depredations.

In the midst of the estate, a vast quarry has been opened, and will be enlarged for the united purposes of procuring stone, and of giving vent to springs, which are here so copious, that from the mouth of the quarry there issues a considerable river, discharging itself with great rapidity, and watering as it flows more than a thousand acres of his richest land.

The highest rocks upon these premises consist of white marble, the lower ones of limestone, and nearer to the level of the sea, there is *tuf*, or a kind of petrefaction, by incrustation of calcareous matter, inclosing the branches and leaves of trees, with other vegetable and animal productions, not marine, but similar to those of the adjacent lands. Descending lower still, near to the sea, we find the surface covered with fragments of schist, and of white quartz.

In this part of his estate, adjoining to the sea, and near to the *Aroyo de la Miel*, he pointed out to me two Roman baths, joined by a Mosaic pavement, and as it appears, formerly covered by the same roof; the one twenty feet long, the other fourteen, each twelve feet wide; the lesser furnished with a stove, and both readily supplied with water, either from the sea, or from the rivulet. The steps to each are twelve feet long, one foot wide, and nine

inches

inches deep. Nearer to the beach appear some vaults, with other fragments of Mosaic pavement.

This enterprising man, a Genoese by birth, is a card-maker, and has an advantageous contract with the government; but happily, being a man of spirit, he employs all his gains in these improvements; and, should he continue to meet with protection from the court, in him it will be seen, that the man, although a stranger, who gives activity to wealth, and calls forth the resources of a country, far from being the object of jealousy and envy, deserves every possible encouragement, and should, as long as it suits him to reside in it, be enrolled among the citizens, and partake of all their privileges.

In his card manufactory, in honour of the marquis of Sonora, he employs two hundred people, to fulfil his engagements with the minister, being bound to supply a given quantity for the service of the colonies. These he delivers at two reals the pack, and government sells them in America for twenty, that is, for a dollar, or four shillings sterling, although better might

might be had for lefs than two pence halfpenny, or one real. In confequence of this extortion, the demand falls fo fhort, that there remain undifpofed of four thoufand boxes, each containing four thoufand packs; yet the contractor continues to deliver the fame quantity as ufual, receiving monthly on account, through Martinis of Malaga, one hundred and fifteen thoufand reals, or eleven hundred and fifty pounds.

There is at Malaga a benevolent inftitution, well fuited to the condition of a country whofe hufbandmen are deftitute of capitals. It is called *Monte pio*, and is in fact a provincial bank, eftablifhed for the purpofe of lending money, without intereft, to farmers, to employ it in the cultivation of their lands. Thefe funds arife from vacant benefices, called *Efpolios* y *Vacantes*. In Gallicia the fame funds are applied in the encouragement and promotion of their fifheries.

The antiquities of this city, with its adjacent country, muft to thofe who have a tafte for fuch purfuits, be highly interefting. It was built by the Phœnicians, and paffed fucceffively under the dominion of

the

the Carthaginians, Romans, Goths, and Moors. The firſt ſovereign who ſwayed the ſceptre there, making it the ſeat of empire, was Haly Abenhamith. When this monarch had eſtabliſhed his power over the kingdoms of Granada and of Murcia, he marched at the head of his victorious troops to Cordova, where, having ſlain with his own hand the uſurper Zuleman, he took poſſeſſion of the vacant throne, and left the united empire to his poſterity.

It was not till the year 1487, that Ferdinand and Iſabella, after an obſtinate reſiſtance, recovered Malaga from the dominion of the Moors. At that period it muſt have been a place of conſiderable ſtrength, and two ſtrong towers, the upper one called Gebalfaro, the other Alcaçava, with their communicating walls, muſt have been the chief dependance of the beſieged. But its antiquities I leave to men better qualified than myſelf to treat of.

Before I quitted Malaga, I enquired into the prices of proviſions. The pound there is of two-and-thirty ounces, but, reduced to ſixteen ounces, the prices were as follow:

Beef,

Beef, twelve quartos, or fomething under three pence halfpenny.

Mutton, fourteen ditto, or nearly four pence.

Bread, five ditto, or not quite three half-pence.

Anchovies, three ditto. Thefe have been fold for one quarto the double pound, but fince there has been a demand for them in Naples, the price has rifen.

JOURNEY

FROM

MALAGA to GRANADA.

ON Sunday evening, April 15th, I prepared, with regret, to turn my back upon a city, with which, upon my first entrance, I was so disgusted, that I determined to leave it the succeeding day. Yet after a three weeks residence, delighted with the manners of the inhabitants, in leaving it I lamented the shortness of my stay. Having then bid adieu to all my friends, and paid the last visit where it was more especially due, to the marquis of Vallehermoso, recommended by his excellency to the care and attention of my guide, I set forwards on my journey.

The

The way, for the space of about three leagues, passes along a bottom, shut in by mountains to the left, but, on the right-hand open to the sea. The whole of this valley is covered with luxuriant crops of corn, as are the adjacent hills with vines. As we advance towards Velez Malaga, the country appears more broken and occupied by innumerable pointed hills, all rich and cultivated to their very summits with the vine. The rock in general is schist, with some limestone, and one hill of gypsum. With such a rich variety of views, it would not be easy to find a more delightful ride than this. At the distance of five leagues we arrived at Velez.

This city occupies a declivity, and is exposed to the influence of the mid-day sun. It is commanded by a castle placed on the summit of the hill, which, as no longer needful for its defence, is suffered to decay. Here are two parish churches, six convents, and, according to the government returns, eight thousand five hundred and twenty-nine souls; but they are supposed to be nearer to twelve thousand.

Much trade is carried on from hence,
chiefly

chiefly for lemons, raisins, figs, almonds, oil, and olives, with some wine.

The government is in a *corregidor*, and thirteen regidores, assisted by the alcalde, alguazil, and thirteen escrivanos.

As to the accommodations for a traveller, I can say little, because I was happy in being received under the hospitable roof of Mrs. Blake, the sister of my banker, Mr. Joyes. Yet from a view of the *posada*, I thought myself doubly fortunate in having secured such good quarters, and such agreeable society.

On Monday, 16th April, at seven in the morning, we proceeded on our journey, passing along the *alameda*, so called from *alamo*, a poplar, this being the tree with which most frequently the public walks are planted. Here, in a cool and refreshing shade, where through the whole year the nightingale sings, and lemon trees diffuse their fragrance, the inhabitants of Velez assemble every evening.

It was with reluctance that I quitted this cultivated spot, where all nature seemed to wear a smile. Here the peasants at every step call for some blessing upon all who pass.

Their

Their manner is soft, their salutation is benevolent, yet peculiar; for they do not, as in other parts of Spain, addrefs the traveller with *vayaufted con Dios*, that is, "God be with you," but *vayaufted con la Virgen*, "May you be under the protection of the virgin."

When we had left this pleafant, this fertile valley, and began to climb the hills, the abundance of goats fhewed clearly the nature of the country, that it was rough, arid, and uncultivated. Such we found it, rugged in the extreme; and if our mules had not been nimble and alert, dauntlefs and perfevering, if they had not refembled in fome meafure the goats, in clambering among the rocks, we fhould never have been able to proceed.

The fcene itfelf was fufficiently terrific, but it was rendered more fo by the frequent view of monumental croffes. Of thefe the moft remarkable was one raifed on the fpot where the marquis S. Antonio and his fervant met their fate. The fituation was convenient for the purpofe, with a fteep afcent, and roads almoft impaffable, to engage his whole attention; whilft fcattered trees

ferved

served to skreen the villains, and enabled them unobserved to fire, at the same instant, on the master and the man.

We had, however, little reason to be afraid, because we had insensibly joined with others in the valley to form a powerful caravan for the passage of these mountains, the usual refuge of smugglers and of thieves. We had a troop of fifty, either horses, mules, or asses; and could have mustered twenty men well armed. Of our company two were equipped more completely than any of the rest; each of these had two guns slung by his side, one very long, the other short; two pair of horse pistols, and two lesser pistols in a girdle, beside a dagger for close quarters, when they should have exhausted their ammunition. These were two officers of the revenue, employed to watch the motions of the smugglers.

One of them, a young man, I found communicative and well informed. He told me, that since the tobacco has been raised from thirty to forty reals, that is, to eight shillings a pound, the smugglers have increased to such a degree, that they have

now

now twenty where they before had one, although the officers wholly employed in collecting the duty on tobacco, are more than eighteen thousand, beside the soldiery, who are often called in to their assistance. He complained most feelingly of the hardships endured by the officers of the revenue, and of the absolute impossibility of living on their pay. This appeared, when he informed me, that for the maintenance of himself and horse, government allowed no more than eleven reals, or two shillings and two pence a day, with an obligation to find his own horse; and, should any misfortune happen, to replace it at his own expence. This speaks for itself, and evidently proves that the most faithful of them all, must have some other dependance beside his pay.

When we had travelled four leagues in about six hours, we arrived at the *puerta*, or summit of these mountains, which were then covered with snow, and after another league, we began descending towards *Alhama*; where, hungry and fatigued, we arrived at four in the evening.

On the heights we had seen only the

cork

cork tree and the ilex; but, in the valley, if with such a rich variety of hills it may be called a valley, we found luxuriant crops of corn.

Alhama is remarkable for situation, being almost surrounded by a precipice, from which you look down upon a river, at least two hundred feet below you. In this it is beautiful to see and hear numerous cascades, assuming various forms, all foaming among the rocks; and when they have spent their fury, gliding almost imperceptibly along in one continued stream. Thus situated, the city is accessible only from the west, where a castle, formerly reputed strong, but now going to decay, commands the entrance.

These rocks are worthy of our observation. The upper stratum is pudding stone. Under this comes silicious grit or sand stone, including broken shells in great abundance; and near the water's edge, at the depth of two hundred feet, there appears a stratum of shingle or rounded gravel. Near to the river are springs, productive of much salt.

Whilst I was considering this singular situation, and contemplating some fragments of the rock replete with shells, an old monk joined me, and, upon looking at my small collection, assured me, as a recent discovery, that what I so much admired was not the production of the sea, but a mere *lusus naturæ*. I thanked him for his politeness, and turned my enquiries towards objects on which he could give me better information. From him I learnt, that the city contained fifteen hundred families, and had three convents, but no kind of manufacture: that mutton sold for two reals, or nearly five pence a pound of sixteen ounces; bread for five farthings; and that as for beef, they seldom if ever tasted it; that the government was in twenty-four regidores, and that the number of *escrivanos* was fortunately confined to four for the service of the city, and of three dependant villages.

As I was walking through some corn fields, I observed the peasants weeding their wheat crops. This operation they performed with very narrow hoes, and a remarkable quick motion. I admired their dexterity, and think their method preferable to our own, as being much more expeditious than that of our English farmers, who,

after

after their spring harrowing, make use of paddles. Were they to employ the same implement among their turnips, they would make no dispatch; and should they exchange it for the hoe among their wheat, they would soon learn to handle it with ease, with expedition, and with safety to their crop.

When I returned to the *posada*, I found a good supper, civil treatment, and a comfortable bed; that is, comfortable, when compared with what I had expected; and in the morning I was equally surprised to find their charges moderate.

Whilst our caravan was assembling and preparing to depart, a venerable monk appeared, with a little image richly dressed, to beg our charitable donations for the *Queen of Heaven*; when instantly every one was eager to express the warmth of his devotion, by kissing her feet, and by giving money to her treasurer. This work of piety accomplished, we began to mount our mules; but we were again delayed for a few minutes, to contemplate an object, which excited horror—the corpse of a poor traveller, who, the preceding night, had been

been robbed and murdered in the mountains, over which we were about to pass. As we advanced upon the mountains, we took notice of many monumental crosses, almost the only objects to be seen upon these unprofitable heights. The intermediate vallies are rich, and many of them well cultivated.

On these *sierras* the smugglers traverse the country, travelling well armed, and in companies of two or three hundred men, with a little field-piece loaded with slugs, and fixed on the saddle of the leading horse. Thus prepared, they have been known to pass unmolested in the presence of the military, when in point of numbers they were by no means equal to a contest.

In this elevated region wolves abound, for which reason shepherds with large dogs keep watch over their sheep by night, and seldom venture to fix their tents at any considerable distance from the fold.

The rock is mostly gypseous, including strata of cristallised selenite.

How striking is the contrast, when, after having traversed these almost barren mountains, the rich and extensive valley of Granada

nada opens on your view. Here, without the affiftance of the Noria, the land is plentifully watered, and loaded with luxuriant crops, fuch as wheat, maize, barley, beans, peafe, hemp, and flax, with vines, mulberries, and olives in abundance.

The conftruction of their plough is remarkable for its fimplicity. The handle, fheet, and fhare, are of one piece. This, with a beam mortifed into it and ftrengthened by a *retch*, with two pins to form the furrow, is the whole implement. Both the handle and the beam are lengthened out by pieces when fuch affiftance is required.

From a comparifon of all the ploughs to be found in the interior provinces of Spain, I am inclined to think, that the firft idea of this now complicated implement originated in the ufe of a crooked ftick, pufhed forwards by a man, to form a furrow in loofe foil. When afterwards he called for the help of oxen, it became neceffary to contrive a beam, in order to regulate the line of draft, according to the ftiffnefs or loofenefs of the foil, and the depth to which he wifhed to move the earth. For this purpofe, it was needful that the beam should be of sufficient length to reach the yoke, that there he might have his point of support to be elevated or depressed, as occasion might require. In process of time he found it convenient to have two pins, to be placed in such a direction on the share as to remove the earth to the right and to the left, and thus to form a wider furrow than the share alone could trace.

Here then we have the plough, commonly used for tillage in the kingdom of *Granada*. As for the fin to the share, the coulter, the fore-sheet, and hind-sheet, the mould-board, the ground-wrist, the drock, the bridle or cat-head, with the foot and wheel or wheels, they are evidently modern, and not yet introduced in this sequestered valley. As for harrows I saw none.

Oxen appear to be the chief dependance of the farmer, both for tillage and for draft. They have no barns either for housing or thrashing out their grain, because when they have reaped their corn, they immediately tread it, on areas in the open fields, with cattle, and having freed it from chaff by the assistance of the wind, they lodge the corn thus cleansed in granaries.

For

For an excellent mule to carry me seventeen leagues from Malaga to Granada, I paid eighty reals, or sixteen shillings, wanting a small fraction.

GRANADA.

GRANADA occupies the banks of two little rivers, the Xenil and the Daro, at the extremity of a vale, the circumference of which is about five and twenty or thirty miles. The valley itself is bounded by high hills, and beyond these to the south is the *sierra nevada*, a chain of mountains, so called because they are covered with an eternal snow. From this circumstance, the south wind is cooled in its passage, and comes refreshing to Granada.

According to the government returns, the city contains fifty-two thousand three hundred and twenty-five souls; but upon good authority, I may venture to say eighty thousand. It is divided into twenty-three parishes, with forty convents, three *beaterios*, seventeen *hermitas* or chapels, nine hospitals, and eight colleges.

Immediately on my arrival, I prefented my letters to the archbifhop, who gave me a polite reception; and, during my ftay, was fo obliging as to make me dine conftantly with him, excepting when I was invited by D. Juan Marino de la Barrera, prefident of the court of chancery.

This metropolitan has an income of two millions and a half of reals, or twenty-five thoufand pounds a year, with which he lives in fome degree of fplendor, maintains great hofpitality, and diftributes largely to objects of diftrefs.

He is well lodged, has good equipages, and is ferved, like other prelates, chiefly by ecclefiaftics, being conftantly attended by his confeffor, chaplains, fecretaries, and pages. The latter are commonly either children of the nobility recommended to his protection, or they claim his favour as being nearly related to the minifters of ftate. In this capacity he has had the nephews of count Florida Blanca, and of the marquis of Sonora.

Thefe pages, when he goes out, attend him to his carriage. When he is at home, they commonly wait in his antichamber, to

receive

receive and to communicate his orders, or at table stand behind his chair. Yet they have time allotted them for study, that when their service is accomplished, they may be prepared for the altar, and qualified to occupy the highest stations in the church.

The confessor, chaplains, and secretaries dine with the archbishop. He is served on plate, has adopted the French cookery, and does well the honours of his table.

His bounty to the poor is such, that we can scarcely conceive his income to equal his expenditure. Beside private pensions to families, and occasional relief in seasons of distress, he provides nurses in the country for 440 orphans and deserted children; he sends poor patients to the hot baths at the distance of eight leagues from Granada, where he actually maintains fourscore; and he daily distributes bread to all the poor, who assemble at his doors. Once, as he did me the honour to inform me, he had the curiosity to count the number of these miserable creatures, and found the men two thousand, the women on that day three thousand and twenty-four; but at another time

time the women were four thousand. In this bounty he is imitated by forty convents, at which are distributed bread and broth, without discrimination, to all who present themselves. The Carthusians alone give annually sixty thousand reals.

These beggars are certainly objects of distress; but the question is, are they proper objects of compassion, and should they be sure to meet with indiscriminate relief? Without it they must perish. With it they propagate the race. Without it they would have no existence. With it they increase and multiply the objects of distress. Surely then charity ceases to deserve that name, when it extends the bounds of human misery. Were it possible to banish poverty and wretchedness by any other means, than by industry and unremitted application, benevolence might safely be permitted to stretch forth the hand, and without distinction to clothe the naked, feed the hungry, give drink to the thirsty, and furnish habitations for the desolate. But the misfortune is, that undistinguishing benevolence offers a premium to indolence, prodigality, and vice. These principles can never be too deeply impreſſed upon the mind. Yet they are ſo little underſtood, that, not merely in Spain, but in more enlightened countries, they are overlooked or violated, and no where more ſo than with us.

In the conduct of our archbiſhop, who is diſtinguiſhed thus by the goodneſs of his heart, and no leſs admired for his underſtanding; I was ſtruck with one inſtance of miſtaken benevolence, not however uncommon amongſt men, as ariſing from our being liable to act under the influence of general principles, without adverting to the reaſons upon which thoſe principles were built. Pleaſed and perfectly ſatisfied with his principal cook, who is likewiſe his confectioner, he was determined to part with this man, rather than advance his wages to ſomething more than five reals, or a ſhilling a day; and this upon a principle of œconomy, that he might have the more to give in charity. Yet this faithful ſervant had a wife and five ſmall children.

One article of his expenditure deſerves the higheſt commendation. It is for free ſchools eſtabliſhed in every part of the dioceſe,

cese, and to these he pays particular attention at his annual visitations.

In one of my visits to the palace, I found him absent, but he had left word for me to follow him. I did so. It was to a jail, where I saw him waiting on the prisoners, and with his own hands serving them, whilst they were seated at a table plentifully furnished. This example of charity he exhibits annually in each of the prisons.

I have observed already, that in compliance with a general invitation, I commonly partook of his hospitality at noon. Besides this visit, few evenings passed without my being present at his *tertulia*, when his friends assembled round him for conversation. Here some of the more ancient amused themselves at cards.

At one of these evening assemblies, I met with a young nobleman, an officer, who had the good fortune to be escorted, in a journey of six days over the mountains, by a party of smugglers, and to find a protector in the very person who had murdered the marquis San Antonio. This man, the captain of a band, was not a robber by profession,

fession, nor did he allow of violence, except in cases of necessity; never permitting his comrades to plunder travellers, unless distressed either for arms, for horses, or for money, after they themselves had been plundered by some officer of the revenue; nor did he suffer them to murder any one, but out of resentment, or for self-defence.

At parting, the young officer would have given money to *Pedilla*, for that was the leader's name, but the generous chief refused it, saying, " When we had the mis-
" fortune to kill the marquis San Antonio,
" it was under a mistake. If you can pro-
" cure our pardon, we will quit a pro-
" fession, of which we have been long
" since weary."

This gentleman assured me, that thieves often rob under the disguise of smugglers, in order to prevent a search, and thereby bring unmerited odium on the illicit trader.

Soon after my arrival, I visited the *alhambra*, or ancient palace of the Moorish sovereigns; and as long as I continued in Granada, I seldom passed a day without returning to contemplate an edifice, so perfectly

fectly different in its ftile of architecture from every thing I had feen before.

You enter firft into an oblong court of a hundred and fifty feet by ninety, with a bafon of water in the midft, of one hundred feet in length, encompaffed by a flower-border. At each end is a colonade. From hence you pafs into the court of the lions, fo called becaufe the fountain in the middle is fupported by thirteen lions. It is adorned with a colonade of one hundred and forty marble pillars. Of this I made a drawing, but had I previoufly feen the beautiful reprefentation of it by Mr. Swinburn, I fhould have faved myfelf that trouble: yet as we have given different points of view, my labour, I truft, will not be loft. The royal bedchamber has two alcoves adorned with columns, and a fountain between them in the middle of the room. Adjoining to this are two hot baths. The great hall is about forty feet fquare, and fixty in height, with eight windows and two doors, all in deep recefles. Between this and the oblong court, is a gallery of ninety feet by fixteen. All thefe lower apartments

have

have fountains, and are paved either with tiles or marble in checkers. The idea of the cielings is evidently taken from *stalactites*, or drop stones found in the roofs of natural caverns. The ornaments of the friezes are arabesque, and perfectly accord with the Arabic inscriptions, which are here suited to the purpose for which each apartment was designed. Thus, for instance, over the entrance to the hall of judgment, is the following sentence:

Enter, fear not, seek justice, and justice thou shalt find.

A handsome stair-case leads you to a suit of apartments intended for the winter.

The *alhambra* has a jurisdiction peculiar to itself, with an alcalde, alguazil, escrivano, prison, gibbet, and a *cuchillo* for the purpose of decapitation.

Adjoining to this residence of the Moorish sovereigns, and communicating with it, is the palace of Charles V. built by Alonzo Berrugete in a superior stile. It has two principal fronts, each of two hundred and twenty feet, by about sixty in height; and the orders are Doric and Ionic, with a rustic basement. The chief entrance

trance is from the weſt under a portal, which has three gates, a large one ſupported by two ſmaller, with intermediate columns and pilaſtres, and battle pieces in baſs relief. Paſſing through a ſpacious hall, you enter a circus of one hundred and twenty-ſix feet diameter, and of a ſingular conſtruction; for it is a cupola, with a periſtyle of two and thirty Doric pillars appearing to ſupport it, but in reality placed there for beauty, becauſe being a cupola it needs no ſuch aſſiſtance. Above this you have a gallery of about twenty feet in depth, with two and thirty Ionic pillars to ſupport the roof; this forms the communication with the principal apartments.

Near to the alhambra is the manſion of the governor, with ſome good rooms, but little worthy of attention. And not far from this, on the declivity of the hill, looking to the weſt, and commanding a proſpect of the city, is the ancient caſtle, with its hanging gardens, furniſhed with numerous fountains, and enjoying a delightful ſhade.

To the eaſt of the alhambra, on the oppoſite declivity, is the old palace of Xenalarife,

larife, which, with its gardens and fountains, may amuse an idle hour, if seen before its more beauteous rival has captivated the whole attention. It is the property of the Conde de Campotejar, a descendant of the Moorish kings.

The ascent towards the alhambra is through a shady and well-watered grove of elms, abounding with nightingales, whose melodious warbling is not confined to the midnight hour: here, incessant, it is equally the delight of noon.

Whenever the heat was too intense to admit of wandering abroad, I took the opportunity to visit churches, and to amuse myself with pictures.

The cathedral, venerable both for antiquity and magnitude, is divided into five ailes, and adorned with Ionic columns. It is four hundred and twenty-five feet long, by two hundred and forty-nine wide; and the great dome is one hundred and sixty feet high, by eighty in diameter. In it are some good modern chapels; and among these the most distinguished is that of *nuestra Señora del Pilar*, of Zaragoza, fitted up at the expence of the archbishop, a native of that city, to be at once the faithful monument of his liberality and taste, and the secure depository of his person and his image. The marble is rich, the sculpture excellent; both are from Italy. To secure the attention of succeeding generations, the materials, and the workmanship, are sufficient of themselves; but to call forth their devotion, the worthy prelate has obtained from Rome peculiar indulgences for those who shall pray before this altar.

Beside this, a chapel behind the great altar, now fitting up, will be, in point of elegant simplicity, a model for all succeeding ones.

Among the best paintings in the cathedral may be reckoned those of Don Pedro de Athanasia, a native of Granada. Of him we admire S. Bernard, a crucifix, the flagellation, the portraits of Ferdinand and of Isabella, with S. Ramon and the blessed Virgin; but above all the famous picture of S. Pedro de Narasco, whose history, if authenticated, would deserve to be recorded. It happened, that when the midnight bell called the fathers of his convent to rehearse their mattins, they were all so sound asleep, that

that not one but himself awoke. As he haſtened towards the chapel, he heard melodious ſounds; and when he entered it, he found the vacant ſeats occupied by angels, and ſaw the bleſſed Virgin in his own, chanting the mattins with more than human fervour.

In the repreſentation of this marvellous event, the painter has exerted his utmoſt abilities, and called forth all the powers of his art.

Beſide theſe, we find four incomparable pictures by Eſpañoleto, two good ones by Riſueño, and one excellent by John of Seville.

Here likewiſe is the famous ſculpture of Charity; and here is depoſited the image of the Virgin, carried by Ferdinand and Iſabella in all their wars, as the pledge of victory.

In the *Cartuxa*, or convent of the Carthuſian friars, every thing is valuable. The pictures are numerous, and executed by the beſt maſters, ſuch as Pedro Perugino, Alonſo Cano, Palomino, Giuſeppe Ribera, called el Eſpañoleto, Athanaſiá, who ſubſcribes himſelf Athaſi, Cottan, a father of this convent, Titian, and the divine Morales. The moſt ſtriking pictures are, for beauty, *Paul*, the firſt hermit, fed by a raven; and, for the marvellous, S. Hugo, holding the ſacramental cup, in which the wine appears to be changed into a little boy. The marbles, in great variety, and highly wrought, are from the vicinity, and appear to be well choſen. Their wine is excellent.

In the church of *nueſtra Señora de las Anguſtias*, is a profuſion of fine marble, with which the mountains in this vicinity abound; but no church in Granada ſhews more want of taſte. The Corinthian pillars, had they been ſimple, would have been admired; but they are deformed by needleſs and moſt unmeaning ornaments.

The other convents, remarkable for good pictures, are Los Angeles, the Capuchins, and S. Domingo. In the cloiſters of the laſt, are repreſented in freſco all the miracles of this ſaint, particularly his reſtoring to life, by the virtue of his roſary, a man who had been two years buried.

San Juan de Dios has a beautiful church, to be admired for its proportions, but to
be

be execrated for abfurdity and want of tafte in all its ornaments. Here the treafures are ineftimable. The urn, in which are depofited the afhes of the faint, is five feet high, furrounded by thirteen images of the apoftles, each of about fifteen inches, and covered by a dome, which is fupported by eight columns of about feven feet high; the whole of maffive filver, and exquifitely wrought.

From the convents I turned my attention to the *hofpicio*, or general hofpital; and, according to the accounts with which I was favoured by the prefident of the court of chancery, who appears to have paid much attention to this inftitution, the whole number of men, women, and children was fix hundred and fifty-five. Of thefe the majority were under the age of fourteen, and the reft chiefly ideots, and people who were become decrepid with old age: yet they are ftated to have earned by labour feventy-five thoufand reals, or one pound two fhillings and eight-pence each upon the average; whilft their food coft only ninety-two thoufand five hundred and twenty-two reals, and their clothing forty-nine thoufand one hundred and eighty-five; the former being equal to one pound eight fhillings, and the latter to fifteen fhillings, that is together only two pounds three fhillings each. If there is no miftake in this account, the greatnefs of their gains, and the fmallnefs of their expenditure, muft be equally furprifing. This account is dated April 21, 1787.

Here is an academy, as in all the great towns of Spain, for the three noble arts of painting, fculpture, and architecture, conducted at the king's expence, and free for all; but this inftitution is yet in a ftate of infancy.

As for the manufactures, they are going to decay, and feel more than the common infirmities of age, receiving at beft little encouragement from local fituation, and being depreffed and ruined by want of political wifdom in the government of this once thriving city. In the year 1552, about threefcore years after the conqueft of Granada, many regulations were publifhed, and afterwards, A.D. 1672, confirmed, laying reftraints on manufacturers, fubjecting them to formalities, and to vexatious fines,

and

and fixing the price at which their manufactures should be sold. As a compensation, the price of provisions was likewise fixed; but as the latter tended to hurt the market, and to depress the farmer, so the operation of the former was to debase the quality of goods, and to bring slow yet certain ruin on the manufacturer, under the absurd idea of favouring the consumer.

The want of political wisdom has been here equally fatal to agriculture, as to manufactures, and to commerce.

At the beginning of the last century, the university of Toledo represented to Philip III. the various grievances by which the nation had been reduced, both as to population and to wealth; stating among these the heavy duties collected in Granada on raw silk, amounting at that time to sixteen reals, or three shillings and two-pence farthing a pound. Don Bernardo de Ulloa, A. D. 1740, makes these amount to nearly seventeen reals and a half, under the various appellations of *alcabala, cientos, diezmos, arbitrio, tartil, torres,* and *xeliz,* terms to be hereafter explained; whereas raw silk was then selling at forty-two reals, so that the tax amounted to more than forty-one per cent.

When Count Campomanes wrote his incomparable work, called *Educacion Popular* the rate, according to the pound, was confiderably higher; but the proportion to the value was diminifhed. He ftates the duties thus. **The** royal tithe, **upon** a fuppofed valuation, is three reals; the ecclefiaftical tithe, collected in kind, now worth fix reals; tartil, feventeen maravedis, or half a real; and the alcavala, $11\frac{32}{34}$ reals; or, in the whole twenty-one reals, fifteen maravedis, equal to four fhillings and three-pence farthing per pound of fixteen ounces: whereas, before the conqueft, the Moors paid no more than three reals and a half, or eight pence three-farthings nearly, for eighteen ounces.

This four fhillings and three-pence farthing was upon the raw materials; but the *alcabala* and *cientos* follow the manufacturer and merchant in all fubfequent transfers of property, till it comes into the hands of the confumer.

The alcabala and cientos have been explained already. *Diezmos* are the tithes;

arbitrio

arbitrio is a tax levied by corporation or municipal government, for provincial purposes; *tartil* was paid to the magistrate, who took charge of, weighed, and sealed the silk in the public magazines; *xelix* was paid to the auctioneer who sold it, and who kept the register; *torres de la costa* is a species of ship-money, for guarding the coasts from the depredations of the Algerines.

It is not possible to think of manufactures in Granada, without calling to mind the expulsion of the Moors, and pausing to examine the policy of that strong or strange measure.

It is universally acknowledged that they were numerous, and that, in consequence of their industry, attended by frugality, they had acquired opulence and power. As to their numbers, we are informed, that of a hundred thousand condemned by the inquisition for apostatizing from the Christian faith, four thousand had been burnt without any good effect. Philip III. in the year 1609, banished to Africa one hundred and forty thousand out of the kingdom of Valencia; and in the three years following,

ing, six hundred thousand from Seville, Murcia, and Granada. If to these we add the multitudes who perished by famine, and by sword, we shall be inclined to state the loss to Spain, at least if not with Count Campomanes at four hundred thousand families, yet at one million of its most active subjects.

This loss, added to what the country had sustained by the previous expulsion of eight hundred thousand Jews, with all their wealth, in the reign of Ferdinand and Isabella, was, under such a government as that of Spain, irreparable.

The Moors are acknowledged, by the best Spanish writers, to have excelled in agriculture, particularly in watering their lands, in the cultivation of mulberry-trees, the sugar-cane, rice, and cotton, all introduced by them; in their peculiar breed of horses, and in the manufactures of silk, of paper, and of gunpowder, first brought into Europe by them.

How then was it consistent with sound policy to subject a country to such a loss? and upon what principles could the sovereign justify his conduct?

Their

Their numbers, their induſtry, their frugality, with their conſequent opulence and power, were circumſtances, if taken in connection with ſome others, which led to their ruin and deſtruction: becauſe, when government conſidered the obſtinate adherence of the Moors to their own religion, their invincible hatred of Chriſtianity, their unity among themſelves in point of cuſtoms, of language, and of creed, and their conſtant correſpondence with the enemies of Spain in Africa; nay, when government regarded them as enemies never to be reconciled, and ſituated in a part of the peninſula naturally not only ſtrong, but moſt acceſſible by a foreign power; their numbers and their wealth were the very circumſtances which made them formidable, and tended to create alarm.

Gentle methods had been tried, more rigorous had been adopted; and, from the time that cardinal *Ximenes* burnt their Alcorans, and baptized their children, they had been ſubject to all the horrors of inquiſitorial power, yet in vain; for their conſtancy was never to be ſhaken, their adherence to the impoſtor Mahomet could

not

not by any means be weakened in the least, much less could it be dissolved. Nothing then remained, but to get rid of them with as little injury as possible to their persons and their property.

In vindication of this transaction, many champions have appeared, and among them no one seems to have paid more attention to the subject than D. Fonseca, in his work called *Justa Expulsion de los Moriscos*. Some of his charges are, however, unworthy of his good sense and gravity, serving only to evince the sovereign contempt in which the Catholic faith was held by the Mahometans. I shall refer to them in order, as they stand, and this chiefly with a view of pointing out the means made use of for the conversion of those infidels. Speaking of the Moriscoes, our author says,

When, being conducted to church by the alguazil, they were compelled to take the holy water, they treated it with every expression of contempt; and when the host was lifted up, *le daban higas por debajo de la capa*; (p. 90.) that is, *they thrust their thumb out between the two middle fingers*; which, in Spain, is the greatest possible indignity,

dignity, and token of defiance. This, however, they did *under their cloaks*.

They neither left legacies in their wills, nor did they give money to procure maſſes for the ſouls of their departed friends, unleſs when compelled to do ſo, and then they came to the prieſt with half a real to purchaſe half a maſs. (p. 92.)

When they were dragged to the confeſſionals, they would not acknowledge themſelves guilty either of mortal, or even of venial ſins. (p. 100.)

Out of twenty children born to them, they carried one only to the baptiſmal font, and him they baptized twenty times, under twenty different names, and even lent this child from one village to another. (p. 106.)

They *ill treated* the images of the ſaints, which they were obliged to receive into their houſes. (p. 128.) That is, ſuch was their abhorrence of every thing bearing the leaſt appearance of idolatry, that, to expreſs their indignation, they forgot good manners; and theſe images were found in the moſt indecent places, with their heads downwards, and other marks of ſovereign
contempt

contempt upon them. (*v.* Geddes Exp. of the Morisc.)

Should the measure itself be vindicated under the plea of necessity, yet the mode in which the expulsion was conducted can never be approved; for the Moors had only sixty days allowed them to dispose of their effects: yet, in quitting the kingdom, they were not to carry out gold, silver, precious stones, unless under the heavy duty of fifty per cent. nor even letters of exchange; but only merchandise purchased of native Spaniards. By their expulsion, houses went to ruin and decay, lands were left uncultivated, commerce was neglected, and manufactures felt the severest shock, a shock such as some scarcely survived, whilst others were wholly lost. The sudden departure of this multitude left a vacuity which it was not easy to fill up, more especially by a nation which, having for the space of seven centuries been trained to war, and inflamed only by military ardour, had learnt in that long interval to look down with contempt upon all who were engaged in the mechanic arts, and more especially to

despise

despise those occupations in which their antagonists excelled.

Numerous privileges and immunities enjoyed by the hidalgos or knights, sometimes called hijos de dalgo, have contributed very much to confirm hereditary prejudices to the detriment of trade. Their depositions are taken in their own houses. They are seated in the courts of justice, and are placed near the judge. Till the year 1784, their persons, arms, and horses, were free from arrest. They are not sent to the common jails, but are either confined in castles, or in their own houses on their parole of honour. They are not hanged, but strangled, and this operation is called *garrotar*, from *garrote*, the little stick used by carriers to twist the cord, and bind hard their loading. They cannot be examined on the rack. They are, moreover, exempted from the various taxes called *pechos pedidos, monedas, martiniegas*, and *contribuciones reales* and *civiles*; that is, from subsidies, benevolence, and poll tax, or taille, paid by the common people, at the rate of two per cent. in this province, but in others at the rate of four.

They

They are free from personal service, except where the sovereign is, and even then they cannot be compelled to follow him. None but the royal family can be quartered on them. To conclude, the noble female conveys all these privileges to her husband and her children, just in the same manner as the eldest daughter of the titular nobility transmits the titles of her progenitors.

The proportion of hidalgos in the kingdom of Granada is not considerable; for out of six hundred and fifty-two thousand nine hundred and ninety inhabitants, only one thousand nine hundred and seventy-nine are noble; whereas, in the province of Leon, upon little more than one-third that population, the knights are twenty-two thousand. In the province of Burgos, on four hundred and sixty thousand three hundred and ninety-five inhabitants, one hundred and thirty-four thousand and fifty-six are entitled to all the privileges of nobility; and in the Asturias, of three hundred and forty-five thousand eight hundred and thirty-three, nearly one-third enjoy the same distinction.

The two high courts of chancery in Spain

Spain are at Valladolid and Granada. The president of the latter honoured me with a statement of the various offices and officers belonging to his court, and subject to his authority. They are as follow:

 16 Oidores, or civil judges.
  8 Alcaldes del Crimen, or criminal judges.
  2 Fiscals, or attorney and solicitor-general.
  1 Alguazil Mayor, or high constable.
  1 Secretario.
 104 Abogados, or counsel.
 12 Relatores de la Civil, or reading clerks.
  1 Teniente Chanciller Mayor; vice-chancellor.
  2 Tesoreros de Penas de Camara y gastos de Justicia, or treasurers.
  1 Contador; accomptant.
 16 Escrivanos de Camara; scriveners or notaries.
  6 Relatores del Crimen; criminal reading clerks.
  5 Escrivanos del Crimen.
  2 Escrivanos mayores de hijos dalgo.

8 Porteros.
3 Agentes de los Fiscales.
40 Receptores, to recover fines.
32 Procuradores; solicitors.
32 Alcaldes de barrio; constables.
　 Alcaldes de Corte.
11 Alguaziles de Corte.
6 Escrivanos de Provincia.
1 Repostero.
1 Alcayde de la Carcel de Corte; jailor.
18 Porteros.

The municipal government is in a corregidor, twenty-four regidores, and twelve jurados, or lord mayor, aldermen, and common-council-men; with two alcaldes mayores, one alguazil mayor, thirty alguaziles ordinarios, three escrivanos de Cabilda, twenty-four escrivanos del numero, thirty-two escrivanos reales, one alcaide de la carcel real, or jailor of the royal prison.

These likewise are subject to the president of the court of chancery.

During my stay in this delightful city I paid several visits to Don Fr. Antonio de Gardoqui, one of the inquisitors, in whom

I found

I found a man of superior talents, well informed, and of remarkable humanity. After I had been one evening with him in his coach, attended by his associate, to take the air in the *paseo* or public walk, the archbishop did me the honour to examine me respecting my feelings; and, in a pleasant manner, asked me, how an English clergyman, a teacher of heresy, could venture his person in a coach between two inquisitors? I told him, that when I had the honour to dine with those gentlemen at his grace's table, I had watched them narrowly, and observed, that they ate *beef* and *mutton* like other men, and concluded thence, that I had nothing to apprehend from them. The idea struck him; he laughed heartily, and assured me, that the inquisitors of the present day were become more gentle than their fathers, and seldom regaled themselves with human flesh; but, said he, look sharp, for they have not yet forgot the taste of blood.

This was true; for although the *Quemadero*, when I went to view it, appeared to be neglected, and was suffered to decay; yet, not more than eight years before, two

Jews and a Turk were burnt upon it; and in the year 1726, the inquisition seized three hundred and sixty families accused of being secretly attached to the Mahometan religion. The accusation, in all probability, was true; because the court of the inquisition, amidst many imperfections, is remarkable for investigating facts; and even to the present day, both Mahometans and Jews are thought to be numerous in Spain; the former among the mountains, the latter in all great cities. Their principal disguise is, more than common zeal in external conformity to all the precepts of the church; and the most apparently bigoted, not only of the clergy, but of the inquisitors themselves, are by some persons suspected to be Jews.

Whilst I was at Granada, I had an opportunity of seeing a wretch hanged for robbery and murder. He had been twelve months under sentence of death, before he was ordered for execution; from that time he remained for some days under the direction of a priest, who gave him instructions, received his confessions, granted him absolution, administered to him the last sacraments,

craments, with the blessing of the church, and left him in the full assurance that, thus prepared, he should go immediately to paradise.

This triumph of christian charity over wholesome policy is universal, and to be found in every part of Spain; where, before the ministers of justice are permitted to execute the sentence of the law, the ministers of grace approach the criminal to administer all the consolations of religion, and to deliver him from the fear of death.

Just as I was entering the *Plaza nueva*, the poor wretch was standing on one ladder, with a halter fastened round his neck, and the hangman from another was preparing to spring upon him. After a few hours, his body was decently interred.

The environs of Granada are delightful; the public walks are pleasant; and the country, all round the city, appears to be well cultivated. Going out one evening by the way which leads to Malaga, and turning to the right, by the *Paseo de Jaraqui*, I wandered among the market gardens. These appear a perfect wilderness of fruit-trees, and yet are covered with the most

lux-

luxuriant crops of all kinds of vegetables. Every cottage has a little court, or bower, formed by a lattice-frame, and wholly shaded by the vine; under which, in the evening, the peasant, with his family, assembles to take refreshment; whilst the nightingale from every tree is uttering his plaintive note. These gardens are all plentifully watered.

Of the public walks, the two most frequented are, one on the banks of the *Genil*, with cooling shades and refreshing fountains; the other, more wild and romantic, by the side of the *Daro*, a river known among the Romans by the name of *Auro*, and so called from the quantity of gold collected with its sand.

In one of my rambles near the *Cartuxa*, I stumbled on a beautiful specimen of schist, carrying iron and white mica, with numerous dodecaedral garnets, brought down from a higher level by the torrent. Ascending about a mile by the side of the ravin, I continually discovered more, and, had not a scorching sun compelled me to retreat, I should have laboured to find out the source from whence they came.

This

This scorching sun is highly beneficial to the production of nitre, at the salt-works near Granada; where, with about one hundred men, employed during the summer, and twenty-six in winter, government obtains three thousand quintals annually. But then the lixiviating water is not carried by men, as in Madrid, but conducted by pipes to every filter.

To procure the proper kind of earth, they observe the spots which, early in the morning, appear black, and towards noon become white round the edges; this they collect, and find that land, on which has been laid much dung, is the most productive. Once collected, it will endure for ages; and, having been exposed to the influence of the sun and of the air, yields the same quantity as at first on every subsequent filtration. In the places where they find this earth, there is neither limestone, chalk, nor gypsum; and, ashes being extremely scarce, none are used at the bottom of the filters.

I have already considered this wonderful production as a merchant; and happy should

should I be, were I qualified to discuss it with any satisfaction as a chemist.

Here a thousand questions crowd in upon the mind. From whence does this earth collect the vegetable alkali, whence the nitrous acid? Supposing the former to be originally the result of putrefaction, yet, after the earth has been lixiviated, and all the vegetable alkali has been carried off by water, how is it impregnated afresh, merely by exposure to the sun and air; and where does it obtain this inexhaustible supply both of the alkali and its combining acid? But, if we reflect, that, with the nitrous salt, there is constantly found muria, or sea-salt, in considerable quantities, whence does it derive the fossil alkali, and whence the muriatic acid, not once, but upon every subsequent exposure?

It is well known that old mortar produces six kinds of salt; for, beside the two just mentioned, both the nitrous and the muriatic acid are found combined with magnesia and with calcareous earth. But, if we recollect, at Añover and Aranjuez we saw Epsom and Glauber's salt, with the

muria

muria and the nitre, and both thofe falts contain vitriolic acid.

Here, then, new queftions will arife. What is the relation between thefe various fubftances, of chalk, magnefia, the foffil and the vegetable alkalis? What connection can we trace between the muriatic, nitrous, and vitriolic acids? and, Is there one common principle of acidity?

This queftion will be both more natural and more interefting, when we confider, as far as relates to England, France, and Spain, the only countries which have come under my obfervation, that, in proportion to the quantity of fun, the chalk is found impregnated with vitriolic acid, and forms felenite or gypfum. At leaft it may be obferved, that in our ifland we have much chalk, and little gypfum; that in France both thefe fubftances abound; whilft in Spain, there is very little chalk, and a profufion of gypfum, more efpecially in Arragon, and in the fouthern provinces. Indeed a learned naturalift, who refided many years in Spain, and traverfed it in all directions, with a view to minerals, affures us, that he had never difcovered there the

leaft

least vestige of chalk. (v. Bowles, p. 13.) But I have already noticed it in one place; and in the neighbourhood of Granada it is likewise found, although I was not able to identify the spot.

His observation is however ingenious, and worthy of attention. He never met with it, I saw it only twice.

The connection between chalk and gypsum became evident to me from the moment that I discovered flinty gravel in the latter, precisely such as we always meet with in the former. Hence it seems to be plain, either that chalk was gypsum, and has lost its vitriolic acid, or that gypsum was once chalk, and has made this acquisition. I am inclined to adopt the latter hypothesis: and, if this be the true one, we must enquire whence has it derived the acid?

Should we be inclined to seek the principle of acidity in the solar ray, we may perhaps be confirmed in this idea by the consideration, that, by means of green vegetables and water exposed to its meridian influence, all modern chemists have produced *vital*, that is *dephlogisticated* air, in great abundance, always in proportion to
the

the quantity of light, or, in other words, to the greater or leffer influence of the folar rays: and that faltpetre, by diftillation, produces the fame kind of air, in the proportion of twelve thoufand inches to a pound, leaving behind the vegetable alkali uncombined with acid.

Should we be inclined to grant, agreeable to the experiments of Dr. Ingenhoufz, that vegetables by day emit vital and by night mephitic air; confidering that Mr. Cavendifh produced nitrous acid by the combination of *vital air* with atmofpheric *mephitis*, in the proportion of feven to three, we fhould not be at a lofs for a never-failing fource, from whence this acid may arife.

Thefe fpeculations might be purfued, and, obferving that one pound of nitrous acid, diftilled on mercury, yields one thoufand eight hundred and eight cubic inches of *nitrous* and one thoufand nine hundred and four of *vital* air, we fhould be confirmed in our opinion that we have difcovered the origin of the fought-for acid.

Nitrous air is obtained from animal fubftances fimply by putrefaction, or it may be had by the combination of *inflammable* and

† vital

vital air: for, as Dr. Prieſtley has remarked, in the Philoſophical Tranſactions of the 27th of November 1788, "When either inflam-
"mable or dephlogiſticated air is extract-
"ed from any ſubſtance in contact with
"the other kind of air, ſo that the one is
"made to unite with the other in what
"may be called its naſcent ſtate; the re-
"ſult will be *fixed air*; but, if both of
"them be completely formed before their
"union, the reſult will be *nitrous air*."

Thus, in the various facts and obſervations above related, we may ſee the intimate relation and connection between inflammable, fixed or mephitic, and nitrous air; that the two latter reſult from the combination of the former with vital air in given quantities; whilſt, with a greater proportion of vital air, we obtain *nitrous acid*; and that, of theſe its conſtituent principles, in warm climates, animal ſubſtances are, by their putrefaction, conſtantly producing one, whilſt vegetables, by day, are as conſtantly pouring forth the other.

In the neighbourhood of Granada are ſome conſiderable plantations of the ſugar-cane,

cane, which, as I am informed, yielded profit during the war; but are now attended with a lofs. Political writers have lamented the lofs fuftained by Spain in the neglect of this once-flourifhing branch of agriculture; as if fome fertilizing ftream had been cut off, or diverted from its accuftomed channel. They would have their country produce every thing it wants, and become thereby both richer and more independent. But in this they forget the benefits of commerce, and the advantages derived by it from the exchange of furplus commodities, when every nation cultivates and produces that for which the local fituation, the foil, the climate, and the genius of the people, are moft adapted. Thus, in the neighbourhood of Granada, the land allotted to the fugar-cane would produce good corn; and the fair queftion is, Since they cannot have them both, which will be moft profitable?

I took notice, in my excurfions round the city, that all the corn-mills have horizontal water-wheels. Thefe are fuited to the country, and on the whole are beft for them.

The

The nature of society I found nearly the same as in other inland situations, where the manners of the inhabitants derive no tincture from intercourse with strangers. The morning is employed, either in business, by those who have any thing to do, or, after mass, in visits to the ladies. They dine early, and eat after the Spanish fashion, with the sopa, the olla, and various kinds of meat stewed in their little pitchers, excepting at the president's and archbishop's, where the French cookery prevails. After dinner they go to the siesta: in the evening to the *paseo*. When the day closes, they assemble at the tertulia, or evening assembly, to which they have access, and here they commonly amuse themselves with some round game at cards.

As for morals, they are much like the rest of Spain: the monks are exceeding corrupt, and the women have no want of lovers to admire their charms. Yet in justice to them I must observe, that, according to the information of Father Porro, a famous confessor, there are numbers who are uncorrupted by the manners of the age, and who excel, not merely in the form but

in

in the power of their religion. These, said he, are not accessible to strangers. Silent and retired, they are scarcely either seen or heard; and therefore, added he, a stranger passing through the country is in danger of being deceived in the judgment which he forms, if he too hastily draws general conclusions.

Before I left the city, I enquired, as usual, into the value of provisions.

Beef sells for nineteen quartos, that is something under five pence a pound of sixteen ounces.

Mutton twenty-three quartos, or nearly six pence halfpenny, in the city; but in the adjacent villages at twelve quartos, or three pence three-eighths.

Bread four quartos and a half, or five farthings and a fraction.

Oil fifteen quartos.

Wine eight quartos the quartillo.

Labourers have four reals, or nine pence halfpenny nearly, per day. Artisans twice as much.

When I was about to leave Granada, my good friend Don Antonio de Gardoqui, the inquisitor, sent me a ham, some chocolate, and

and six bottles of old wine, as my stock of provisions for the journey.

The distance from Granada to Carthagena is computed to be fifty leagues; and for a good mule to carry me I agreed to give two hundred reals, or forty shillings nearly, being at the rate of five shillings a day; not allowing for the return, because the mule belonged to the *corsarios*, or public carriers.

Thursday, 26th April, we left Granada. Near the city the hills are cultivated and covered with vines; but, as we advance, the country becomes more wild and broken, with high and rugged rocks laid bare and destitute of soil. The intermediate plains are abandoned to the Esparto rush, or stipa tenacissima of Linnæus, the quercus coccifera, the juniper, and a few miserable ilex.

The rock is chiefly schistous, often covered with limestone; and the surface is scattered with white quartz, which seems to have been formed in the schist, where it appears in considerable veins.

On these high mountains we saw many monumental crosses: but not one is recent, because,

because, the police being here well established, and the laws now put in force, robberies are seldom to be heard of, and no murder has been committed the last twenty years.

After having travelled about six leagues we came to a village among the mountains, comprising about one hundred and seventy families. It is called *Diezma*.

As I travelled the whole day fasting, I hastened to the butcher's to see what was to be had. There I learnt the price of provisions, and found that mutton sold usually for twelve, beef for eight quartos (two pence farthing) the pound of sixteen ounces; bread for six and a half. For wine I paid three quartos the quartillo. But, unfortunately, neither beef nor mutton were to be had; and, to fill up the measure of my consolation, at the *posada* I could obtain no bed, nor yet a room.

What could be done? The day was closing, and it began to rain. The alcalde was to be sought for; but he was no where to be found. At the end of a long search, I met him returning from the field, and, after a short salutation, presented him my pafs; yet to little purpofe, for he could neither write nor read. We went next in purfuit of the *efcrivano*, but he was not at home. At laft, however, we found a peafant, who had learnt to read and write. The pafs was produced, and fubmitted to an accurate examination. It required, that I fhould be provided with *every thing needful*, at a reafonable price.

The alcalde having liftened to it with attention, enquired what I wifhed to have. I replied, a bed. A bed! no fuch thing is mentioned in the pafs. But, if *your mercy* will have the goodnefs to obferve the expreffion, *every thing needful:* no, no, a bed is not *needful* to a traveller; he may do very well without one. I told him, with great humility, that it was for *his mercy* to judge of what the pafs implied, and began quietly to retire; when, feeming to recollect himfelf, he ordered a billet to be made out.

With this I went to my deftined cottage, where a bed was fpread upon the floor, and I went fupperlefs **to reft,** having had little for the whole day but fome hard eggs, and, for want of a cork-fcrew, fuch wine only

as

as the vineyards in the neighbourhood produced.

The next morning the good people of the houfe prepared my chocolate; and, when I was to take my leave, no perfuafions could prevail on them to accept of money for my bed.

From *Diezma* we began defcending, and foon came into a fpacious plain, bounded on the fouth by the mountains of the Sierra Nevada; rich in its foil, but too far removed from habitations to admit of cultivation, and therefore abandoned to the efparto rufh. From this plain we continued to defcend by the fide of a wide and deep ravin, in which appear many horizontal ftrata of rock, feparated from each other, ten, fifteen, and even twenty feet, by beds of clay, fand, and gravel. Having left the ravin, we came to a little village, called *Parillena*, fhut in by high cliffs of the fame materials, with fome beds of unmixed gravel. Here many of the habitations are merely excavations in the earth.

At night we came to *Guadix*, having travelled from Granada twelve leagues by computation, or, as I conceive, about fifty miles.

All the way on the right, towards the Sierra, the country has a moſt ſingular appearance, looking like the ſtormy ocean; and the innumerable pointed hills ſeem to have attained, what may be called their quieſcent ſtate, being no longer fretted, waſhed away, and ravaged by heavy rains and vernal torrents. Protected by herbage, they are now fed by every ſhower, and at this ſeaſon of the year exhibit a delightful verdure.

It is evident, that the formation of theſe hills is of recent date, and ſubſequent to the general revolution, which took place when the horizontal ſtrata, for ages covered by the waters of the ocean, were lifted up to view, and became the habitable portion of our globe. At that period, the whole of this country appears to have been one extenſive plain; but, being compoſed of ſoft materials, and ſubject to violent and heavy rain, it was ſoon torn in every poſſible direction by gullies, which, in proceſs of time, became deep ravins, till, the mouldering angles of high cliffs being waſhed away,

away, the wide expanse was left covered with hills, whose pointed tops, as we may here observe, are all on the same level.

The elevation of this country is so great, and such is the influence of the adjacent mountains, covered with eternal snow, that the vineyards shew no signs of vegetation; whereas at Malaga, eighteen days before, they were covered with leaves and fruit.

Guadix, situated at the foot of the Sierra Nevada, is a considerable city, and a bishop's see. It is divided into five parishes, and contains eight thousand three hundred and fourteen inhabitants, with seven convents, five for monks, the other two for nuns.

At the entrance to the city is the *alameda*, or public walk, well planted, and remarkable for neatness.

The *cathedral* exhibits three orders of architecture, Corinthian, Composite, and Anomalous. The front is whimsical, yet pretty. The inside is Doric and Corinthian. The marble, from the vicinity of this city, is beautiful, and of various colours, red, grey, white, and green.

There are here some manufactures of hemp, flax, and silk; but the situation is far from being favourable to them. The article for which this city is most celebrated being pocket knives, the first attention of my guide was to purchase one; and when we set forwards on our journey the succeeding day, he produced it.

The blade was sixteen inches long, and, when open, it was prevented from shutting again by a strong spring. Although this was the first of the kind I had ever seen, my imagination immediately suggested the purpose for which it was designed. Having produced his weapon, he began to brandish it; then, supposing himself to have been suddenly attacked by some one, armed with an implement similar to his own, he stooped forwards, bending his knees, and holding his hat before him, by way of shield, in his left hand; whilst his right hand, depressed and grasping hard the handle of his knife, directed its elevated point. Thus prepared, and casting a look of fury on his supposed antagonist, he sprung forwards, and, appearing to have received in his hat the thrust of his opponent, he gave the fatal blow, which was to enter at the lower belly,

belly, and in one inftant to rip up the miferable wretch from end to end.

These knives are ftrictly forbidden; but, unfortunately, inveterate cuftom is too powerful for human laws, more efpecially in a country where the paffions are eafily inflamed; and where, from the nature of the judicial procefs, the laws muft be weak in the extreme. For, as we have remarked already, no information can be taken but by the *efcrivanos*, nor can any judgment be pronounced but upon their record. Now, as thefe officers are ufually poor, and not unfrequently deftitute of principle, they may, without much difficulty, be perfuaded to change the complexion of an action, and at pleafure to make it either black or white. Hence, from impunity, affaffinations are frequently committed; and, as little fecurity can be derived from the laws, it becomes the intereft of every man to be armed for his own defence. With this view only he procures the formidable weapon; but, when provoked to anger, his views are changed; that which was defigned for his own protection, becomes the inftrument

ment of treachery, of malice, and of revenge.

Throughout this elevated country, there is little appearance of cultivation, although many confiderable tracts of land, over which we paffed, are good, and much of it might be watered. The natural productions are pines, juniper, favine, rofemary, with other aromatic herbs, Spanifh broom, and the *paſſerina hirſuta*, but chiefly the *eſparto* rufh.

Whilſt traverſing theſe mountains, the fnowy tops of which are loft in clouds, we obferved many flocks of goats, fome of them numerous, and one confifting of five hundred; but we faw no fheep. As we advanced we met nine waggons, and a long drove of affes, loaded with flax, going to Granada. The leader in thefe droves is always diftinguifhed from the reft, and will never fuffer another to ufurp his place.

The waggoners and drovers were all affembled, and, being feated on the grafs before the doors of a *venta*, that is, a folitary inn, were eating for their dinner fome fnails dreffed with rice. As we approached, one of them refpectfully rofe up, and invited

vited us to partake of their repaſt. We as reſpectfully declined the offer, and proceeded to another venta, at the diſtance of about four leagues from Guadix.

Near this place I had an opportunity of obſerving the ſtrata, and found them compoſed promiſcuouſly of quartz, flint, ſchiſt, and limeſtone gravel, all rounded as by the action of water.

The *trillo* was ſmaller than any I had ſeen before; and, inſtead of flints, had forty bars of iron to cut the ſtraw.

Soon after we had left this venta, we began deſcending by the ſide of a *baranco* or ravin, and with the higheſt ſatisfaction entered the rich vale of *Baza*. Yet even here the vines had not begun to bud.

Baza is ſaid to contain ſix thouſand five hundred families. The cathedral is ſcarcely worth attention. The organ indeed is large and handſome; but the great altar is antiquated, and void of taſte.

Below the city is an extenſive well-watered plain. The ſoil is very white, and, although remarkably ſtrong, is tilled with the plough laſt deſcribed, without either coulter, fin to the ſhare, or mouldboard;

yet

yet the wheat appears tolerably good, but the barley is very bad. They plough with mules.

From hence, afcending for near two leagues, yet ftill traverfing the fame plain, which is bounded every way by fnowy mountains, in a circumference of about thirty miles, we difcovered, that through this whole extent of country the natural rock is gypfum, and from that circumftance arifes the whitenefs of the foil in the fubjacent plain. The ftrata appear to be horizontal, and are many of them compofed entirely of double lenticular cryftals of felenite, like thofe of Montmartre, in the vicinity of Paris.

Nitre is remarkably abundant over the whole extent of this gypfeous country.

On Saturday, April 28, in the evening, we came to *Cullar de Baza*, a wretched village, with many habitations excavated in the rock of gypfum. Previous to our departure, the fucceeding day, it was indifpenfable that we fhould go to mafs.

Here I obferved, that, as the chapel was not fufficiently capacious to receive all the people who attended, many ftood on the outfide, outside, where they could neither see the officiating priest nor hear his voice. When, however, the sound of a little tinkling bell had reached them, they smote upon their breasts, and, having crossed themselves, their devotions for that day were ended. Being at liberty to spend the remainder as they pleased, some began to amuse themselves with sports and pastimes, others worked in their gardens, and some went out to plough.

The little valley, which supplies this village, is about a quarter of a mile in breadth, inclosed by barren gypseous mountains; and although it is well watered, and consequently fertile in flax, hemp, and wheat, with vines on the more elevated spots, yet the population bears too great a proportion to the extent of land susceptible of cultivation.

Looking down upon so rich, yet such a contracted spot, we instantly and evidently see that the human race, however at first, and whilst their numbers are limited, they may rejoice in affluence, will go on constantly increasing, till they balance their quantity of food. From that period the appetites

appetites will combine to regulate their numbers. Beyond that period, should they continue to increase, having passed the natural limits of their population, they must suffer want. In these circumstances, beholding many of the poor, naked, and half starved, should they inadvertently ordain, that no one in their community should want, that all should have food, and every man an habitation; or, in other words, should they establish a community of goods; is it not obvious, that they would aim at impossibilities, and that, by every effort to relieve distress, they would only extend the bounds of human misery?

This subject is highly interesting, and should be thoroughly discussed; but, as I have treated it professedly in a Dissertation on our Poor Laws, and often occasionally in this work, I shall drop it for the present.

All the way from Cullar de Baza to *Vertientes*, three tedious leagues, we keep winding among the hills, which are covered with rosemary and aromatic herbs, but chiefly with the esparto rush and a few straggling pines. Here we saw no sheep. The

The whole country is given up to goats; of these we admired one flock, containing two thousand, all as white as milk, feeding among the rocks, and scattered on the sides of a high mountain.

As we approached the puerto, or pass, we observed a few sheep among the goats, and some droves of pigs feeding round the scattered ilex.

Vertientes, so called from the parting of the waters, has twenty-five families; and *Contador*, at a little distance, has twenty more.

Beyond this pass the prospect opens, and, in proportion as we descend from the high country, where the waters divide, one portion passing by the Daro to the Xenil, and thence by the Guadalquivir into the ocean; whilst the other, by a shorter passage, is precipitated with the Guadalentin, near Carthagena, into the Mediterranean sea. In proportion as we descend, vegetation begins to feel the influence of a warmer sun; the soil becomes more fertile, and all its productions appear luxuriant. The esparto rush, which in those elevated regions could scarcely be distinguished

guished from grafs, at a lower level becomes long and rampant. The vines begin to shoot, the lark is warbling in the air, and throughout a wide-extended valley the crops every where promise an abundant harvest.

At the distance of more than *a league* from *Vertientes*, or, according to the expression of my guide, *a league as long as Lent*, is *Chirivél*, a village containing a hundred and fifty houses, which, with fourteen others, including all the adjacent country, and one third of the tithe, is the property of the Dutchess of Alba. Here they have neither beef nor mutton; goats flesh sells for ten quartos, or $2\frac{13}{16}$ pence a pound of sixteen ounces; and bread for two quartos and a half, or $\frac{45}{64}$ of a penny.

From hence we descend three leagues in the wide channel of a torrent, shut in by high hills and rugged rocks of schist, all the way to *Velez el Rubio*, where the country again opens on the view, and the vale expands.

This town is said to contain three thousand families, with one solitary convent, and a beautiful church, built by the
Dutchess

Dutchefs of Alba, to whom the town and the adjacent lands belong.

The Pofada makes a magnificent appearance, and, for a Spanifh inn, may be called commodious; but, confidering the expence the Dutchefs has been at for the advantage of the public, more attention fhould have been paid to the comfort of genteeler travellers. The rooms, deftined for their reception, are of a good fize, and communicate by means of a fpacious gallery. But the whole of the ground floor is abandoned to the carrier, and confifts of a fmall kitchen, with a vaft repofitory, defigned at once for the lading of their mules, for their entertainment, and for their dormitory. Here their noife and riot, refounding through the houfe by means of the long gallery, is intolerable; and, as the kitchen is open, they are conftantly crowding round the hearth to procure their fuppers, leaving the miftrefs of the pofada no *leifure* to pay attention to any guefts befide themfelves.

The town is commanded by a caftle formerly ftrong, now going to decay.

They have no beef. Mutton is fold for

twelve

twelve quartos a pound, ($3 \frac{5}{16}$ pence), goats flesh for ten, bread for four.

From Velez you pass over an open and a fertile plain, till you reach the confines, and from the kingdom of Granada enter Murcia. Here the prospect changes; and, instead of a level country productive of grain, and not destitute of fruit-trees, you meet with nothing but hills, barren, wild, and desolate, the resort of wolves, covered chiefly with the esparto rush.

To guard this pass, a castle, called *Xixena*, formerly a place of strength, was erected on the summit of a craggy rock, and its ruins still preserve a respectable appearance. The rock is schist.

As we drew nigh to *Lorca*, we overtook numerous droves of asses, loaded with pine-wood, cleft for the service of the hearth; and observed the Tamarisk, with the Nerium Oleander in great abundance.

Here the soil is white, and the gypsum rock appears.

After having passed three days in these elevated regions, constantly in sight of snow, and exposed to the severity of the winter's cold, the sudden transition to the

heat

heat of summer, as we descended into the plain, was more striking than agreeable. No sooner were we arrived near Lorca, than we observed multitudes of swallows, and when we came into the city, we were pestered with myriads of flies. On the mountains vegetation ceased, whilst at a lower level the peasants were engaged in the toils of harvest.

The hardships to be endured in the journey from Granada to Lorca, can be fully comprehended by those only who have passed this way. With respect to living, it is bad; with regard to lodging, it is worse. I had indeed taken the precaution, or rather my friend the inquisitor had the goodness to provide a ham, and six bottles of good wine, but to little purpose; for unfortunately the ham had been neither boiled nor watered; and in this whole extent of way, and indeed in the whole tract of country between Granada and Carthagena, no vessel could be found big enough to boil it in, nor any thing deeper than a frying-pan. At Cullar de Baza I had ordered it to be dressed; and a traveller, who had joined me on the road, recommended that it it should be boiled in wine. I gave orders accordingly, and I paid for the wine; but when, in the morning, I attempted to cut some slices, I found it was raw, and upon examination, found that my ham had been for hours over a little bit of fire, and in a vessel fit only for the frying of eggs. My wine occasioned equal perplexity, for I had no screw, and could neither procure a fork to draw out the cork, nor was there room to thrust it in. Patience, and a penknife, however, at last relieved me from this part of my distress.

The first night of my journey I was so happy as to be in a place, where my passport could procure a bed; but in a succeeding night, being at a *venta*, had not the good gypsies, for such they were, spread their own for me on the floor, I could have found no resource. They indeed at first refused; but when they saw that I was ill and fainting, they took compassion, and with cheerfulness resigned the bed, reserving, however, for themselves the chamber in which it had been spread.

But in Lorca, after having regaled myself with a good supper, and slept soundly in a
comfortable

comfortable bed, I forgot all former hardships.

Lorca is a considerable city on the banks of the Guadalentin, and contains, in nine parishes, twenty-one thousand eight hundred and sixty-six inhabitants, with eight convents for men, and two for women. It had lately manufactures of silk, wool, and linen, but these are gone to decay. Should the canal, intended to run up into the country, and to form a communication with Carthagena, be carried into execution, trade will revive, and agriculture, by the watering of more than three hundred thousand acres of good land, will receive fresh vigour; for such is the effect of moisture, in this warm climate, that, in a rainy season, the farmers have received a hundred for one upon their wheat.

The salt-petre works are here extensive, and appear to be conducted at a small expence of fuel.

I was delighted with the public walks, resembling the parks at Oxford, but upon a more extensive scale, and more beautiful, because the corn-fields, inclosed by them, are watered. Here, in the evening, the inhabitants affembled to take their exercife, and to enjoy their focial intercourfe under the fhadow of the lofty trees.

The parade for the militia is fpacious, and after fun-fet affords a pleafant walk.

Of the convents, thofe moft worthy of attention are S. Jago, S. Domingo, and La Merced.

The great church has nothing remarkable within, excepting a curious grant from the bifhop and the dean, of forty days indulgence every time any penitent fhall fay a pater nofter and an ave maria to fix faints, named in the grant, provided this be done for the benefit of the fouls in purgatory.

The front of this church is elegant, the columns numerous, the architecture is Corinthian and Compofite. Here every criminal may find a fafe afylum.

An old caftle, ftanding on the edge of a high rock, formerly the object of dependance, or of terror, is now regarded with indifference.

As we traverfed the plain, after having turned our back upon this city, we took notice of the tillage. The land is ftrong,

the

the ploughs are similar to the one last described, and in these are used two asses. With such apparently bad husbandry, how astonishing must be the influence of the sun, to produce upon their watered crops of wheat a hundred-fold in proportion to seed!

Near the city we remarked olives in abundance, with many mulberry-trees; and took notice of numerous flocks of sheep, but saw no pens for them. The shepherds were attended by strong dogs, armed with spiked collars, whence I collected that wolves find shelter on the mountains.

My guide talked to me of some lead and copper mines in this vicinity, but I had no opportunity to visit them; yet I saw clearly, by the nature of the mountains, that minerals must abound in them.

As we increased our distance from Lorca, we lost sight of cultivation, and ascended among hills covered with esparto rushes, yet not altogether destitute of other vegetable productions, such as are more pleasing to the sight. Among these, the principal were the *spartium*, or Spanish broom, the nerium oleander in a few favoured spots, the *passerina hirsuta*, and the lovely cistus in abundance.

The soil is white with gypsum; yet the rocks on the mountains to the right and left appear to be of schist. Nitre, both on the hills and in the vallies, might be collected in the greatest plenty, and at a small expence.

Here the peasants wear short trowsers, and buskins, called by them alpargates, which are made with the esparto rush. Of these a man is able to manufacture two pair a day, and requires for his own use one pair every fortnight, being at the rate of about twelve shillings a year for this article of dress: whereas in Granada, where the shoes are made with hemp, and cost three reals, a pair will last three months, being at the rate only of two shillings and four pence per annum.

After having travelled seven leagues, we came to a village, called *la Penilla*, containing fifty scattered cottages; it is situated on the elevated tract of land, which is interposed between the two vales of *Lorca* and of *Camponubla*. The soil is calcarious, and produces, of wheat, eight for one; but

of

of barley twenty-four for one. A few mulberries, figs, olives, and prickly pears, by their luxuriant growth, serve to shew what the country, if duly cultivated, is able to produce. The barley is already housed, and the wheat is nearly ready for the sickle.

The land lies healthy, without the least sign of stagnant water; the springs are more than a hundred feet below the surface, and the inhabitants are remarkable for being free from tertians and from putrid fevers, whilst the vallies suffer exceedingly from both.

They have here no great proprietor, nor *vinculo*, as they express it. That is, the estates are freehold, and not entailed. Nothing, therefore, is wanted but a market to promote their industry. Bread sells at four, and mutton for ten quartos the pound.

We left la Penilla at six in the morning, and traversing a level country, shut in with high mountains and craggy rocks of schist, we came to the pass, and from thence descending to enter the vale of Carthagena, beyond the summit of the hill, we lost the

limestone

limeſtone for near a league, and found the ſchiſt; but, leaving that behind us, we again met with calcarious earth and limeſtone, whilſt all the higher rocks are evidently ſchiſt.

Near the ſummit is a noria, with water at the depth of ten feet from the ſurface.

Wedneſday, May 2, I arrived at Carthagena, about the middle of the day, and found a moſt hoſpitable reception in the family of Mr. Macdonell, an Engliſh merchant eſtabliſhed there.

CARTHAGENA.

CARTHAGENA occupies the declivity of a hill, with the little intermediate plain between it and the harbour. This city is protected from the south and from the west by high mountains and barren rocks; but to the north and to the east it is open, and communicates with an extensive valley.

This valley, as we have seen, is separated from the plain of Penilla by a ridge of hills, which is a continuation of the mountains above mentioned; whilst, to the north, another chain of mountains divides between it and the vale of Murcia.

On the summit of the hill, commanding the city, is a castle now going to decay; but, on the adjacent heights, are raised considerable works to defend the harbour, with the arsenals and dock-yard.

They

They reckon here sixty thousand souls, distributed in fifteen thousand families.

The streets are wide, and the houses are commodious. They have generally flat roofs, which, in a climate like this, administers to the comfort of the inhabitants, affording them a cool retreat, where, after sun-set, they may assemble to enjoy the refreshing breeze; and, as the rainy season is of short duration, these are sufficient to protect the interior of their mansions from humidity. The new parade, extending east and west at the head of the harbour, and looking through its entrance into the Mediterranean, is built on a regular plan: and, as a high schistous rock has been cut away to make room for this long range of habitations, excellent vaults are excavated behind each house, for the service of the merchants. At the end of this stands the royal hospital, a vast establishment, destined to receive the sick from the dock-yard and the army, with the *presidiarios*, or criminals condemned to the gallies, and in Spain reduced to the lowest state of servitude.

The cathedral, a miserable pile, is now degraded, and the bishop's see being removed

moved to Murcia, it is become a parish church.

Of the convents not one appeared worthy to be noticed; but the proportion allotted to the men is certainly remarkable; becaufe, of nine, eight are occupied by them. Yet I could not learn the reafon for this neglect and want of provifion for the fex, whofe helpleffnefs, whether in the ftate of orphans or of widowhood, pleads powerfully for fuch a refuge; and who by nature are moft fuited to the devout and peaceful engagements of the cloifter.

I wifhed to have vifited the dock-yard: but, when I left Madrid, knowing that I fhould meet Mr. Macdonell, I neglected to folicit letters of recommendation, and, for want of an order from the court, I was not able to procure admiffion. My lofs, however, was the lefs to be regretted, becaufe I had vifited the arfenals at Cadiz, and becaufe every part of this dock-yard may be diftinctly feen, either from the adjoining hills, or from the houfes, which look down upon it.

In the midft of the yard is a fpacious bafon, and in it the fhips of war are moored, ed, each in front of the magazine deftined to receive her rigging and her ftores.

The docks are kept dry by fire-engines, and of thefe, three are almoft conftantly at work. Confidering the enormity of this expence, it appeared to me, that by means of water they might raife a fhip to the needful height, and then fuffer the fire-engine to reft till water was required to let her down again.

They have here two thoufand criminals, chiefly fmugglers, who, being condemned to work in chains, are called *prefidiarios*. Thefe are employed in the moft fervile labour, fome for five, others for feven years; and at the expiration of thefe terms, they are turned loofe upon the public, not corrected nor trained to habits of induftry, but vitiated by the fociety of thieves, and unfitted to purfue the occupations to which they had been originally trained. Before the introduction of fteam-engines, thefe wretched creatures were obliged to work at the chain pumps; but fuch was their malignity, arifing from defpair, that many, watching their opportunity, would throw ftones, stones, nails, and bits of iron, into the pumps, to spoil them.

These two thousand slaves require five hundred soldiers constantly to guard them; and, independently of this expence, they cost each to government five reals a day for their maintenance; whilst their work cannot be estimated at one-tenth of what they eat.

This absurd practice of employing convicts in the public service, is no longer confined to Spain. We have adopted it in our more enlightened island, as may be seen at Portsmouth, where the master general of the ordnance finds employment for two or three hundred criminals, who are better fed than the most sober, honest, and laborious of our peasants. Their daily allowance amounts to more than eighteen ounces of bread, with nearly a pound of butchers meat, an ounce of cheese, a quart of soup, nearly a quart of beer, and plenty of potatoes. Thus fed, with good clothes, a comfortable lodging, and light work, is not their condition to be envied by the industrious poor? Yet such, to the nation, is the expence, that the

charge

charge for each individual is more than sufficient to maintain a family.

If, at Carthagena, we calculate the allowance for their convicts, omitting the soldiers pay, we shall find thirty-six thousand five hundred pounds expended, beside what is spent for the same purpose in the other sea-ports and garrisons of Spain. Yet, notwithstanding the enormity of this expence, and the cruelty thus exercised on the persons of those, who, under a wiser government, might have been profitable citizens, such is the effect produced by a vicious system of finance, that neither are these reclaimed, nor are others intimidated from treading in their steps; whilst, with regard to the revenue, not merely is little gained in proportion to what is taken from the public, but, by the subtraction of such multitudes from profitable employment, their labour is lost to the community.

In this dock-yard the masts and timber are floated in water, without the least apprehension of their suffering by the worm; because, as they never open their sluices till the water is become putrid, the evaporation,

tion, proceeding with rapidity, leaves a strong brine, in which it is impossible the worm should live; whereas, in the north of Spain, where the evaporation is not sufficient for this purpose, they bury their masts in sand, and by pins prevent their floating, when they are covered by the tide.

The fishery at this sea-port is considerable. It is divided into two branches, perfectly distinct and independant of each other; that within the port being the property of a fishing company, consisting of eighteen associates, established here by charter, whilst, in the open sea, all mariners, who are enrolled, are at liberty to fish.

Within the port they take chiefly the atun, or tunny and the *melvas*; but the former is the most profitable. It is from five to seven feet long, in shape somewhat like a mackarel, but the head is large and the tail is very small; the flesh is brown and flaky and admits of being salted. By this they clear about ten reals, that is two shillings, per arroba, or one penny, nearly, a pound. The melvas are purchased by the

regidores

regidores for sixty reals, that is twelve shillings, the hundred.

Half the quantity of fish taken in the harbour must be sold for the benefit of the poor, at a price appointed by the regidores; and the king takes one-half of all their profits, amounting to about a thousand pounds a year, as a compensation for his claim of one quarter of their fish. They are not allowed to follow their occupation in the night, lest they should take that opportunity for smuggling. In addition to these impediments, the regidores take the best fish themselves, at their own price; and, whilst they purchase at sixty reals, they sell again at a hundred, dividing the plunder among themselves. Till the year 1750, the corregidores, alcaldes, and regidores, claimed the privilege of taking the best fish without paying for it, under the title of *bostura*, that is, a bribe or recompense for fixing the price; but, by a royal edict, that practice was prohibited; and now, if they resolve to plunder, it must be circuitously.

In the open sea the fishermen enjoy more freedom from oppression, and have peculiar privileges.

privileges. Their fresh fish is disposed of in the market, free from the alcavala, millones, arbitrio, and every other tax, only subject to the regulations above related, by which their profits are reduced; but as a compensation, for their salt, supplied from the royal magazines, they pay one real per fanega less than others to the king, and have six months credit. They export their salt fish duty free; and for home consumption, whilst foreign fish pays ten they pay only two per cent. in lieu of alcavala and millones to the crown. Yet they complain of being plundered by the intendant of marines, from whom they are to obtain their licence, and allege that he likewise robs them of their fish.

The magistrates, if called upon by the fish-carriers, must fix a reasonable price on baskets, casks, and package, and must determine what shall be paid for the weighing of their fish.

Here they make great quantities of the *esparto* ropes and cables, some of them spun like hemp, and others platted. Both operations are performed with singular rapidity. These cables are excellent, because

Vol. III. K they

they float on the surface of the water, and are not therefore liable to be cut by the rocks on a foul coast. The esparto rush makes good mats for houses, *alpargates* for peasants, and latterly it has been spun into fine thread for the purpose of making cloth. If properly encouraged, there is no doubt that the manufacture may be brought to such perfection, as to make this once useless rush a source of abundant wealth to the southern provinces of Spain.

We have remarked, this rush, as the peculiar and natural production of all the high and uncultivated mountains in the south; and here we cannot help admiring the bounty of providence in thus administering to the wants of man, and giving abundantly in these dry and elevated regions, where neither hemp nor flax will grow, materials proper for his clothing, and for the employment of his industry.

The Spanish government, in order to derive a revenue from this valuable article of commerce, began, A. D. 1773, with laying a duty of two and a half per cent. on the exportation of the manufactured rush, and nine maravedis per arroba on the raw material.

material. But some few years after, willing to confine the manufacture altogether to their own subjects, they proceeded further, and forbad the exportation of the raw material; yet, unmindful of their favourite maxims, they have given to John Baptista Condom, of Madrid, a licence, nay an exclusive privilege, of sending it to a foreign market.

The most important production of this country, and the most valuable article of commerce is barilla, a species of pot-ash, procured by burning a great variety of plants almost peculiar to this coast, such as *soza, algazul, suzon, sayones, salicornia,* with *barilla*. It is used for making soap, for bleaching, and for glass.

All the nations of Europe, by the combustion of various vegetable substances, make some kind of pot-ash; but the superior excellence of the barilla has hitherto secured the preference. The country producing it is about sixty leagues in length, and eight in breadth, on the borders of the Mediterranean.

The quantity exported annually from Spain is about a hundred and fifty thousand quintals,

quintals, paying a duty of seventeen reals per quintal, consequently producing a revenue of twenty-five thousand five hundred pounds a year: yet, as we are informed by Don Bernardo de Ulloa, A. D. 1740, this article was farmed at six million two hundred and sixty thousand four hundred and twelve maravedis, that is £.1,822. 4s. 3d. Were it not for this oppressive tax, the quantity exported might be much increased, because the French, who formerly frequented the Spanish markets for barilla, are now supplied from Sicily, where, next to Spain, the best may be procured.

Carthagena is indebted principally to M. Macdonell for this article of commerce; at least to him must be attributed the flourishing condition to which it has been brought, because, previous to his establishment in this city, little of it was produced in the vicinity, and none was transported from a distance.

All the herbs already mentioned, as yielding the pot-ash, are indigenous, and may be collected in a swamp called *Almojar*, to the eastward of the city. Of the soza I found two species, the one called *blanca*,

the

the other *fina*. These are both good, yet not equal in quality to the *fayones* and *barilla*.

The chief imports are bale goods and bacalao; the latter directly from Newfoundland, under the duty of thirty reals the quintal, or about six shillings the hundred weight. Of bale goods, muslins and cottons are prohibited; yet as many are now brought in as when the ports were open to them, government suffering thereby in the revenue, and the people paying double the former price for these commodities.

In my excursions round the city, I took notice, that the extensive valley to the north, and to the east, is beautifully varied in its form, every where either rising into little tumuli or sinking into bottoms; and although not enriched by any rivers, yet, from a few scattered norias, it is evident, that even the highest land might be plentifully watered. The soil is loomy, composed of calcarious matter, sand, and clay, from the dissolution of the adjacent mountains, which are of schistous rock covered with limestone.

They use oxen for draught; but in tillage

lage they employ mules and asses, with the plough last described.

Their course of husbandry is wheat, barley, and fallow. For wheat they break up their land in September, and, after three ploughings, the seed is put into the ground about the middle of November or the beginning of December. In July they reap from ten to a hundred for one, in proportion to the wetness of the season. For barley they move the earth once or twice, as opportunity permits, sowing their land generally in September, but always after the first rain subsequent to the wheat harvest, and receive from thirty to forty fanegas of grain on a fanega of land, or, in other words, from fifteen to twenty for one upon their seed, because a fanega is that quantity of good land, on which they sow one fanega of wheat or two of barley.

A fanega of corn is here three thousand three hundred and twelve solid inches, and weighs a quintal, that is, one hundred pounds Spanish, or one hundred and two pounds and three quarters avoirdupois; and among the merchants five fanegas and a quarter are reckoned equal to eight Winchester bushels of

two

two thoufand one hundred and feventy-eight folid inches; but upon a rough calculation, two fanegas of grain may be reckoned equal to three bufhels, and one fanega of land may be confidered as three quarters of an acre.

For their fallow crop they often fow barilla, and get from ten to twelve quintals on a fanega; but if, for want of rain, they are difappointed in the proper feafon for wheat, they fow that land likewife with barilla; and fuppofing the market price to be forty reals the quintal, it is found more profitable than a good crop of wheat. The average price is confiderably higher; but as the commodity rifes and falls between wide extremes, it is fometimes fold for twenty, and at other times for a hundred and twenty reals the quintal.

They grind all their corn by wind-mills. I counted thirty near the city; and water is fo fcarce, that M. Macdonell pays thirteen pounds a year only for the carriage of it.

The trees moft common in the valley are, elms, poplars, olives, figs, pomegranates, mulberries, apricots, palms, palmitos, and the ginjolero. This laft bears a little fruit refembling, both in fize and form, the olive, but with a fmaller kernel, and remarkable for sweetness. The leaf is something like the ash, but of a darker green, with a shining surface.

The palmitos *(Chamærops humilis)* grow about two feet high, with leaves on a long stem spreading like a fan. They bear good dates in clusters, and the root is excellent, resembling the artichoke. Between each coat is a fine texture of fibres, like network, commonly used instead of hemp for charging and for cleaning guns.

I have remarked already, that the rock is schist covered with limestone; but in some places we find the silicious grit or sand stone, with shingle or smooth gravel and sea-shells; and at no great distance from the city is a mountain, from whence they obtain the gypsum used for plaster. The whole country abounds with saltpetre.

✓ Of diseases, the most endemical are intermittent and putrid fevers. These arise from the proximity of an extensive swamp, containing many hundred acres, which might easily be drained, so as to produce the most luxuriant crops. In the year 1785, during the three autumnal months, they lost two thousand five hundred persons, and the succeeding

ceeding year two thousand three hundred more; yet the Almojar remains undrained. Government, indeed, exerted its authority, but not in the most effectual manner, for the relief of the inhabitants.

When the report of this calamity had reached the court, an order was dispatched to the physicians, that no other medicine should be administered to the sick, than the famous one prescribed by Don Joseph Masdeval, and called by him his Opiate, of which the following is the formular:

℞ Sal absinth,
— Ammoniac optime depurati āā ʒi.
Tartari Stibiati, termino clariori Tartari Emetici gr. xviij. triturentur per horæ quadrantem, deinde adde & optime misceantur Pulv. Cort. Peruv. ʒi.
Syr. absinth q. s. fiat Opiata.

Of this he gives one-sixth part every two hours, with one spoonful of the following mixture:

℞ Aq. viper ʒv.
Aq. benedict Rulandi termino clariori Vini Emetici ʒj.
Cremor Tartari pulv. ʒj. m.

With

With these medicines he interposes plenty of broth, and continues to use them till the patient is restored to health.

In a conversation I had with him at court, he informed me, that the common operation of these medicines was at first to act as an emetic or cathartic, often bringing away lumbrici; but being continued they relieved the stricture on the external surface of the body, promoted perspiration and acted sometimes as a diuretic. He assured me, that in the most desperate cases, the disease had given way at the end of four days, after he had begun to administer his medicines; and he did me the honour to shew me a variety of attestations from medical men, in almost every part of Spain.

That I might have no doubt of the true nature of the disease, he related the usual symptoms, such as, in the beginning, a remarkable prostration of strength, with intense pain both of the head and of the back; intolerable thirst; the tongue foul, dry, black, chopped, and trembling, when protruded; pulse small, hard, quick, and intermitting; parotid glands swelled; urine limpid

limpid at firſt, but turbid in the progreſs of the diſeaſe; reſpiration difficult; the white of the eyes become red; petechial ſpots on the arms and breaſt; hands trembling; watchfulneſs at firſt, followed by propenſity to ſleep perpetually without conſciouſneſs of having ſlept; delirium; noiſe in the ears, followed by deafneſs; involuntary tears; coldneſs of the extremities; quivering of the under lip; and, if the patient were ill treated, death.

From this deſcription, there could be no doubt of the diſeaſe; but, as to the operation of the medicines, that certainly will admit of ſome diſcuſſion. On the common principles of chemiſtry it is evident, that a double decompoſition takes place, and that the tartar emetic is reduced to an inert calx. I muſt acknowledge, that when firſt I was informed of this curious medicine, I was inclined to think, that the tonic power of the bark enabled the ſtomach to bear this extraordinary quantity of tartar emetic, but on more mature conſideration it ſeems clear, that, being decompoſed, this active medicine has loſt its efficacy; and I am confirmed in this idea by

a fact

a fact related to me by Dr. Mafdeval, when I had the honour to meet him at the Efcurial. He had prefcribed this opiate to a monk, who was in the laſt ſtage of a *typhus* or putrid fever; but the nurfe by miſtake gave the whole quantity at once, thus adminiſtering eighteen grains of tartar emetic at one dofe, yet without any other vifible effect than abating the violence of all his fymptoms. I am therefore fatisfied, that the cleanfing of the alimentary canal muſt be attributed to the emetic wine, and that the operation of the famous opiate would be nearly the fame either with or without the ſtibiated tartar, and muſt be afcribed wholly to the bark.

The phyficians of Carthagena were willing to allow this medicine all the credit which was due to it, and to prefcribe no other whenever they fhould be convinced that this might be ufed with fafety; but to be precluded in all cafes from the ufe of other remedies, they thought, would be unreafonable. They therefore fent their remonſtrances to court; but in anfwer, there came an exprefs order from the king, that they fhould be fubject to the intendant of

the

the dock-yard, and should prescribe according to his directions.

On the receipt of this mandate from the court, the intendant immediately assembled the physicians, and made known the royal pleasure, informing them, that in case of disobedience, the prisons were prepared, and the guards in waiting to execute his orders. They expostulated, but to little purpose; and being told that nothing short of absolute submission would be accepted, they consented to prescribe the opiate in all cases, and, to evince their sincerity, they signed a certificate, that no other medicine was so efficacious as this recommended by the king.

The people, however, were not so submissive to the royal mandate, and knowing that the physicians were engaged not to vary their prescriptions according to the exigency of the case, and the variety of diseases by which they might be attacked, they absolutely refused to send for medical assistance, and resolved to take their chance for life or death. When therefore information was carried back to court, that the physicians were likely to be starved, and the people

to die for want of their advice; the minister
relented, and agreed to compromise the matter, leaving the sons of Æsculapius at liberty
to follow their own judgment for the citizens at large, and compelling them to administer no other medicine, beside the opiate,
to all the patients in the royal hospital.

This perhaps is the first instance of despotic power controlling the functions of physicians, and prescribing uniformity to that class
of citizens in the line of their profession.

The municipal government of Carthagena is in a military governor, with his alcalde mayor, thirty regidores, whose office
passes by inheritance, if not previously sold,
and two syndics, chosen by the people as
their peculiar guardians.

The governor is the supreme and independent judge for the army, and for strangers settled in the country, whilst his alcalde
presides in the tribunal for the citizens.

Nothing can be more vicious than this
form of government by hereditary regidores,
who may here be called the thirty tyrants:
yet to render the yoke still more intolerable, the *escrivanos del numero* succeed likewise by inheritance, and may even sell their
office

office in fhares, to be ferved by a deputy. Although the *fyndics*, like the Roman tribunes, are chofen by the people, it is under the influence of the regidores; and as they are appointed only for a year, they dare not exert themfelves in the difcharge of their duty towards their fellow-citizens.

It is reported, that in confequence of this vicious fyftem, both the *regidores* and *efcrivanos* are conftantly intent on plunder. Certain it is, that many fources of peculation are open to the former, befide the one already mentioned, in fetting a value on provifions; but the principal, and thofe, moft generally noticed, are, creating new offices for themfelves or their dependants, with more than ample falaries, and diftributing among themfelves large fums under pretence of deftroying locufts, where few or none are to be found; after which they make falfe reports to government, and procure fuch vouchers for their watchfulnefs, activity, and zeal, that they obtain high encomiums when they deferve the moft fevere reproof. Not long fince, they expended three hundred thoufand reals, or about three thoufand pounds, and then levied

vied the whole by an *arbitrio* or tax on the inhabitants, although no one could imagine what part of the adjacent country had been infested by the locust. To complain of these abuses would be dangerous; and to such an extent is the venality increased, that every citizen is anxious to secure the favour and protection of a regidor, as the only means of safety for his person and his property. This circumstance is sufficient to evince the viciousness of government, and the mal-administration of the laws; for wherever patrons with their clients are to be found, we may be certain that the laws are weak, and that violence hath usurped the throne of equity.

In consequence of this want of energy in government, murders and assassinations are frequent in Carthagena, and for many years not one offender has been punished for these crimes, because the most atrocious villain, unless miserably poor, may find refuge in the rapacity of the *escrivanos*.

Want of fidelity to matrimonial vows is equally prevalent at Carthagena, as in the other provinces of Spain.

It

It was here that a gentleman one morning said gravely to his friend, "Before I go to rest this night, the whole city will be thrown into confusion." This he himself occasioned by going home an hour before his usual time, to the no small vexation of his wife and of her cortejo, whose precipitate retreat, and unexpected arrival in his own house, occasioned the like confusion there; and thus by succeffive and similar operations, was literally fulfilled the prediction of the morning.

I have already traced the corruption of morals to one grand source, the celibacy of the clergy; but here it must be observed, that this operates only as a pre-disposing cause; whilst the occasional cause, by the acknowledgment of those, who are most competent to judge, must be sought for in the introduction of Italian manners on the arrival of Charles III. from Naples, with the previous want of reasonable freedom in the commerce of the sexes.

If in addition to these I might venture to assign another cause for this universal depravity of morals, I should seek for it in the want of admonition; because the secular clergy

clergy feldom, if ever, preach. The monks indeed defcant upon the virtues of their patron faint; or labour to extol fome favourite feñora, and to fet up altar againſt altar; but they feldom appear folicitous to improve the morals of the people; and excepting during Lent, they do not often exhort the people to repentance. Their contemptible effufions have been juſtly ridiculed by a Spaniſh author, who, in point of wit and humour, has had few fuperiors; and all who have read his entertaining hiſtory of the famous preacher, *Fray Gerundio*, will acknowledge the juſtneſs of his cenſure. Had not this work been moſt abſurdly condemned by the inquifition, the fame reformation might have been effected in their pulpit eloquence, as was happily produced in England by a fimilar performance of our Echard, entitled, " Grounds and Occafions of the Contempt of the Clergy."

Such has been the poverty of Spain in point of pulpit orators, that neither monk nor ecclefiaſtic, among all with whom I converfed, could recommend one author, as worthy to be noticed; and even in the
prefent

present day, if a preacher of more than common abilities appears, he is admired as a prodigy, and almost worshipped as a saint.

Precisely such was a famous capuchin, Father Diego, of Cadiz, who visited Carthagena whilst I was there, and every evening preached in the great square to more than ten thousand people. Many of his admirers assembled early in the morning to secure good places, but as he did not begin till after six, the magistrates gave orders that no one should be allowed to take a seat till two in the afternoon; yet finding the tumult and confusion, the broken chairs and broken heads, thereby increased, they permitted every one to use his own discretion, and consequently, some more zealous than the rest, again took their stations soon after sun-rise.

The good father is learned, eloquent, and modest; and although the vulgar ascribe to him a variety of miracles, he disclaims all such pretensions.

This man, licensed by the bishop, and protected by the magistrates, was constantly attended by a guard, to prevent his clothes
from

from being torn from his back for relics. What he spoke was heard with the most profound attention; and after one discourse on the forgiveness of injuries, many were reconciled, and became good friends, who had been before at enmity. One sermon, however, had a pernicious tendency; yet so deeply is a sense of honour, of gratitude, and of filial piety impressed on the human heart, that few appeared to relish his doctrine, or to be convinced by his arguments; but most of his hearers seemed to shudder with abhorrence, when he endeavoured to persuade them, that in cases of heresy, they were in duty bound to accuse, at the tribunal of the inquisition, their nearest and their dearest friends.

Before I left the city, I enquired into the price of beef and mutton; the former was sold for twelve, and the latter for thirteen quartos the pound of sixteen ounces.

A quarto is one farthing and an eighth English.

JOURNEY

JOURNEY

FROM

CARTHAGENA to ALICANT.

ON Tuesday, May 15, at seven in the morning, I took leave of my obliging friends, and set out for Murcia in a calasine; and traversing the vale by which I had entered Carthagena, at the distance of four leagues, I came, about noon, to the *Venta de Jimenao*. After dinner, in about three hours, we left the valley, and ascended by a beautiful new road among the mountains, most of which are cultivated to their very summits.

The reason of this, and of the extraordinary fertility of the vale from which we had ascended, appears to be the constant mouldering of the high and tender schistous rocks, by which the soil is renovated and fed unremittingly with a rich and loamy clay.

By cutting through the hills to make the road, they have discovered vast strata of shingle or smooth gravel, of white quartz, of limestone, and of silicious grit.

As we ascended, we met two waggons loaded with garlic, and my guide assured me, that what I saw was the weekly supply for Carthagena.

In descending towards Murcia, I took notice of one monumental cross, and by the inscription, it appeared that a traveller had, three years before, been robbed and murdered there.

The vale of Murcia is equally rich, and rich from the same cause as that of Carthagena; but it certainly exceeds in beauty every thing I had seen in Spain. The soil is a rich loam, well watered; and the wide expanse appears like a well cultivated garden. Oranges and lemons, olives and mulberries abound; and the whole valley swarms with such multitudes of men, all active and usefully engaged, that they resemble bees, when employed in collecting honey, or returning loaded to the hive. Being

ing dressed in white they are the more conspicuous; they have only a linen waistcoat, and short trousers.

As we approached the city, one of the *corsarios*, or common carriers, who accompanied us all the way, had the misfortune to break a basket committed to his care, and thereby the greater misfortune of discovering the contents. After this accident I observed him pensive, and evidently saw, that although tempted, he at first resisted his inclination. At length he took one cake, closed the basket, and turned away his eyes; but by degrees he seemed to get the better of his scruples, and before we reached the city, he had almost cleared the whole. Had he met with the temptation sooner, I am inclined to think that not one cake would have arrived at the place of its destination. I smiled at his simplicity, and pursuing my reflections on the various temptations incident to human frailty, I arrived at this conclusion, that ignorance of evil is the best guardian of our innocence.

The entrance to Murcia is by a straight and spacious avenue, well planted, and well watered; to the right and to the left of which the land, with water in abundance, produces the moſt luxuriant crops.

The city is divided into eleven pariſhes, with a cathedral; and contains, by the laſt returns to government, fifteen thouſand families. It has nine convents for nuns, and ten for friars.

As ſoon as I arrived, I haſtened to the cathedral, whoſe lofty tower had, from a great diſtance, attracted my attention. The front is elegant, with ſixteen marble columns of the Corinthian order, and thirty-two images as large as life. One of the moſt ſtriking features about this edifice, is a chapel of the Marquis de los Veles, an hexagon, covered with a dome, in the Gothic taſte, which is both light and elegant. Round this chapel is a ſtone chain curiouſly wrought.

I was much diſappointed when I entered the cathedral, to find the interior of it ſo little correſpondent to the expectations excited by the beauty of its front. Indeed there is nothing in it remarkable, beſide the pictures and the jewels.

Of two ſilver altars, one is plain; the other, for high feſtivals, is more ornamented.

mented. One *custodia* of silver, for the elevation of the host, or consecrated wafer, weighs nearly six quintals and an half, that is, something less than six hundred weight; another contains eight pounds and four ounces of the purest gold, with six hundred emeralds, and many valuable diamonds. One vessel somewhat similar, only used for preserving the consecrated wafers, and called *el copon*, has five pounds of gold, beside many brilliants of considerable value. On the right-hand of the altar is a massive urn of silver, four feet long, two and a half wide, and four feet high, containing the ashes of the two bishops, Fulgentius and Florentinus. Over this, a little chest of gold and silver, highly wrought, contains one hair taken from the beard of Christ, and sent from Rome by Cardinal Velluga, who was bishop of this diocese.

It would be endless to enumerate all the jewels belonging to this church, forming a mass of treasure, which, if in circulation, would animate the general industry, and be productive of new treasures to the country, as far as its influence could extend.

The sacristy allotted for the reception
of

of this wealth, is in the centre of a vast tower, constructed like that of Seville, but at present not quite so high. When finished it will be more lofty by ten feet than that famous edifice. As you ascend, not by steps, but by inclined planes, you go round the sanctuary, a spacious apartment destined as a refuge for assassins, where they may be equally secure both from the sword of justice, and from the dagger of revenge.

In this voluntary prison I saw two murderers, who had each his bed. They attended me up the tower, and appeared happy to converse; but I had so little expectation of hearing truth, that I did not urge them to relate the circumstances which brought them to that melancholy dwelling.

From the top of this high tower you have a delightful prospect, commanding all the valley, with the circumjacent mountains. From hence you look down upon the city, every way surrounding the cathedral, and itself placed nearly in the centre of the vale; the dimensions of which, extending east and west, are nearly six leagues,

and

and two leagues from north to south. It is bounded on the south by the chain of mountains over which we had passed, and by which it is separated from the vale of Carthagena. To the east it communicates by a small opening of about a league, with the vale of Orihuela and the sea. To the north-west are hills, and beyond these, high mountains bounding the distant view.

The cathedral is built with freestone, distinguished by the name of Pisolite, because it appears to be composed of shells in small fragments, with round globulæ, resembling the spawn of fish. It contains likewise many bivalves and anomice entire.

Of convents, the largest is that of the Cordeliers, but the prettiest is the one allotted to the nuns called *las Capuchinas*.

I was exceedingly struck with the bridge over the *Segura*, magnificent in itself, and delightful for the prospect it commands of the river, the city, the vale, and the distant mountains, all in the most pleasing points of view.

This river being often overflowed during the rainy season, the city would have been long since swept away, had it not been for
a strong

a strong dike, twenty feet wide, and as many high, by which it is protected. This dike, projected merely for the safety of the city, being extended many miles up into the country, affords a pleasant walk to the inhabitants; and as they have fixed here the sacred *stations*, it serves likewise the purpose of devotion. I have already explained the nature of these stations, when describing the convent of the Francifcans at Seville.

No one, who has lived always in a temperate climate, can conceive how much a traveller suffers from the flies, when he passes the summer in the southern provinces of Spain. But of all the cities through which I passed, not one appears to be molested with such swarms of those teasing insects as Murcia. It is here, therefore, that a man may fully comprehend why Beelzebub, god of the flies, should become the title of a being, who is held in supreme detestation by the human race. To disperse them, in some houses, they have a large fan, suspended over the dining table, and kept constantly in motion; in others, one of the domestics is unremittingly engaged

gaged in waving the bough of a tree all the time the company is eating; but the great, have a servant at their elbow, whose sole employment is, with a napkin, to keep off the flies.

My stay was short in Murcia. This city, with its environs, is highly interesting; but unfortunately, not finding the letter of recommendation to the principal person in his native city, with which Count Florida Blanca had favoured me, I too hastily concluded that the custom-house officers at Cadiz had lost it, when they examined my portmanteau, and took from me all my letters. I had afterwards the mortification to discover, that they had placed it among my letters to Valencia; but it was then too late to profit by the discovery. Disgusted with the filth and miserable accommodations of the posada, and having no other recommendation to any person resident in Murcia, after having passed one night in it, I resolved to quit the city.

The posadero, who, like most of the innkeepers in this part of Spain, is a gipsy, assured me, that he paid thirty reals, that is, six shillings a day for rent, and seven
hundred

hundred and fifty reals a year for alcavala; yet among all the wretched ventas and pofadas I had seen, this appeared one of the most wretched.

His composition for the alcavala is very low, because every arroba of oil, paying five reals, and the pound of butcher's meat three quartos, supposing his consumption to bear any proportion to his rent, the amount must be considerably more than seven pounds ten shilling per annum.

Notwithstanding these heavy duties, *beef* sells for eleven quartos, or a trifle more than three-pence the pound of *sixteen* ounces; *mutton* for thirteen quartos; *pork* is worth fifteen; *kid* sixteen; *bread*, if very white, four quartos.

On Wednesday, May 16, at three in the afternoon, I placed myself in my calasine, and proceeding by the river side, took the road for Alicant.

To the left is an old castle on the summit of a high calcarious rock, which is insulated, pointed like a sugar loaf, and charged with extraneous fossils.

All the crops, such as wheat, barley, oats, peas, flax, hemp, with alfalfa *(medi-*

cago

cago sativa) appear luxuriant, and the trees are full of verdure. These are chiefly the elm, the poplar, the willow, the cypress, oranges, lemons, figs, mulberries, palms, medlars, quinces, and pomegranates. In short, the whole valley is one continued garden.

I took notice that all the ovens are separate from the cottages, and are covered with earth to retain the heat.

Early in the evening we arrived at *Orihuela*, four leagues from Murcia. It is a rich and thriving city, built on each side of the Segura, and contains twenty one thousand souls, with thirteen convents, and a seminary for two hundred students, established here, A. D. 1555.

The cathedral is antiquated, and little worthy of attention; but the parish church of S. Augusta is elegant; and that of the Augustin friars will, when it is finished, be a valuable acquisition to the city.

In the neighbourhood are established some good saltpetre works for government.

Water in the whole of this valley is so abundant,

abundant, that the crops have no dependance on the rain: hence the proverb,

Llueva o no llueva, Trigo en Orihuela.

From this city we paffed along the valley, with the river on our right, and high mountains to our left, through vaft plantations of mulberry trees. Here, the liquorice appears as a noxious weed, fpreading over the whole country; becaufe the foil, being deep, is peculiarly fuited to its growth; and the warm fun, with plenty of water, makes all vegetables fhoot with peculiar vigour.

The rock is calcarious.

Leaving this extenfive plain, with the Segura on the right, we turned up a little vale of communication to the left, and paffing between high rocks, at the end of about a mile, we entered the rich vale of Punda. This, with many correfponding vallies, all run from eaft to weft, agreeable to the general direction of mountains and vales in Spain, and near the fea communicate with the vale of Orihuela.

On the mountains we obferved fome monumental croffes.

The

The dress of the peasants consists of a waistcoat, trousers, stockings, all white; esparto sandals, a coloured sash, and a close black bonnet.

At the distance of two leagues we came to *Alvatera*, a miserable village, with a magnificent church, belonging to the Marquis of Dos Aguas. The country produces chiefly vines and olives. As we advanced we met a travelling flock going to feed upon the mountains. At the meeting of four roads we took notice of a high pole, with an iron hook, supporting one quarter of a man. The other quarters were suspended in the principal places where this wretch had been guilty of robbery and murder.

In the bottoms, the wheat crops appear heavy, and bowing for the sickle; and the barley is collected round the areas ready to be trodden by the cattle.

All the roads are here in a state of nature; but were the rich soil of clay and loam removed, a firm bed of gravel would be uncovered, and the roads for many generations would want no repairs.

At the distance of about a mile from Elche, passing the wide bed of a torrent, then

then dry, at the entrance of an extenſive grove of olives, I obſerved three poles, ſimilar to the one I had remarked before, each with the quarter of a man, being the monuments of as many robberies, accompanied with murder.

Elche, Ilici of the Romans, might with propriety be called the City of Dates, for it is every way ſurrounded by plantations of palm-trees. Theſe, about the month of May, are loaded with fruit in pendant cluſters, which, forming a complete circle, reſembles, when ripe, a crown of gold, with a plume of feathers riſing from its centre. Each cluſter to appearance would nearly fill a buſhel, and is ſaid to weigh from ſix to ten arrobas. There is a remarkable variety in this fruit, both as to the taſte and colour. Some dates are green when ripe, but moſt commonly they are yellow, and not unfrequently of a dark brown. Some are ſweet, others are inclined to acidity. The male trees produce only flowers, the females bear the fruit.

Elche is divided into three pariſhes, and contains, according to the laſt government returns, ſeventeen thouſand four hundred

and

and three souls, of which eight thousand six hundred and fifty-seven are males, and eight thousand seven hundred and forty-six females; but the widows are seven hundred and fifty-one, and the widowers three hundred. They have twenty knights, eighteen advocates, twelve escrivanos, thirteen inquisitors, and three convents, two for monks, the other for nuns. The great church is a beautiful building, with a majestic dome, and is elegantly fitted up. For the service of the altar it has two curates, a vicar, four doctors, and many chaplains. It is built with sand-stone; but as the natural cement is weak, the stone moulders away and cracks.

This city belongs to the Duke of Arcos, now Count of Altamira. It is governed by his corregidor, four regidors, as many deputies from the commons, two alcaldes, and one alguazil mayor. The ducal palace is situated on the brink of a deep ravin, and carries the marks of the most remote antiquity. It was recovered from the Moors by Peter surnamed the Cruel, A. D. 1363.

They have no beef. Mutton is sold for thirty-

thirty-two quartos the pound of thirty-six ounces; lamb for twenty-three; pork for thirty-six; wheaten bread is worth five quartos and a half the pound of eighteen ounces, and barley bread two quartos.

Leaving Elche, and paſſing through conſiderable plantations of olive-trees, interſperſed with algarobos, when the proſpect opens, you have the ſea on your right-hand, at the diſtance of about a league; on your left you ſee the diſtant mountains fading on the ſight, and ſinking in the horizon; whilſt at the diſtance of four leagues in front you command the high fort of Alicant.

As you approach towards the city, the country is wild and broken, diſcovering a ſandy rock; but having deſcended nearly to the level of the ſea, you find a rich ſoil, and luxuriant crops of corn, with extenſive plantations of the almond.

In all the ſouthern provinces of Spain, eſpecially in this vicinity, you ſee numerous fountains and reſervoirs of water covered with arches, all, though perhaps unjuſtly, attributed to the patient induſtry of the

the Morifcos; when, with equal probability of truth, they might be afcribed to the Romans, to the Carthaginians, or to the more ancient inhabitants of the peninfula.

I was much entertained in this fhort journey with the fuperftition of my guide; a fpecies of fuperftition not confined to him, becaufe I found it equally in all the coachmen and common carriers with whom I had afterwards occafion to converfe upon the fubject. They carry conftantly about with them the paw of a mole, to fecure their mules and horfes againft the *mal de ojos*. This I at firft conceived to be the *difeafes of the eye*; but upon a more accurate enquiry, I found myfelf miftaken, and difcovered that this expreffion meant, the evil influence of witchcraft, conveyed by looks. In the fouthern provinces of Spain, like as formerly in England, and even now in Cornwall, children and the common people univerfally agree in attributing necromantic powers to the female in each village who is the moft deformed in perfon, the moft decrepit with old age, and the moft haggard in her looks. In Cornwall it is needful for the witch thrice to repeat, " I wifh;" but in Spain one look conveys the fatal influence; and the object, unlefs relieved by a fuperior power, may droop and die. The proper amulets are the paw of a mole carried in the pocket, a bit of fcarlet cloth worn by men, or the *manefita* faftened on the wrift of children. The manefita is a little hand of jet, ivory, glafs, or ftones, fet in filver, with the thumb thruft out between the middle fingers. But for want of thefe, a perfon apprehending danger may readily defend himfelf by the fame pofition of his thumb. For this reafon, whenever the fond mother obferves an ugly hag looking fteadfaftly upon her child, fhe fcreams out, *fefta una figa*, that is, thruft out the thumb in token of defiance.

In this little journey I took notice of a new eftablifhment, which does much honour to Count Florida Blanca, as contributing not only to the eafe and comfort of the traveller, but to the fafety of his perfon. Government is engaged in raifing, at the diftance of every league, a little cottage, with a fuitable garden, as the habitation of

a *peon*

a *peon caminero*, who is to receive five reals a day for repairing the highways, and for protecting paſſengers. For this purpoſe he is furniſhed with all proper implements and arms. This inſtitution will be made general through all the provinces.

ALICANT.

ALICANT is situated at the bottom of a bay, formed by the capes of La Huerta and San Pablo. It is protected by a castle, built on the summit of a mountain, to which, when attacked by enemies, the citizens have been taught to look up with confidence; but, in the present day, it is rather the object of their terror, because large portions of the rock, shattered exceedingly, overhang their base, and threaten a part of the city with destruction.

The streets are narrow, and were exceedingly ill paved; but now, indebted to the indefatigable zeal of the governor, don Francisco Pacheco, few towns can boast of superior neatness; and by the well directed labours of one man, this city, formerly in every sense a nest of vermin, is become a most delightful residence.

By the last returns to government it appears, that the inhabitants are seventeen thousand three hundred and forty-five. Of these, eight thousand five hundred and twenty-four are males, eight thousand eight hundred and twenty-one females; the unmarried men and boys, four thousand nine hundred and sixty-six; the unmarried women and girls, four thousand five hundred and seventy-six; but the widows, nine hundred and thirty-seven, whilst the widowers are only three hundred and forty-one. Divided according to their age, there appears to be:

Under seven years of age, males and females	2,865
From seven to sixteen	3,144
From sixteen to twenty-five	2,870
From twenty-five to forty	3,782
From forty to fifty	2,033
From fifty upwards	2,651
Total,	17,345

The clergy are fifty-six, including those, who in four parishes have the cure of souls, with others who are ordained either to ecclesiastical

clesiastical benefices, or on their private patrimony; this being equal to three reals a day, that is, to about eleven pounds sterling per annum.

Of the seculars, sixty-four are knights, twenty-eight advocates, thirty-one escrivanos, two hundred and ninety-four students, nine hundred and seventy-four farmers, two thousand three hundred and one day-labourers; the merchants and shopkeepers are three hundred and thirteen; the manufacturers, eleven; the artisans, one thousand three hundred and ninety-two; the servants, six hundred and thirty. Beside these, eight convents contain about two hundred and fifty persons under vows.

The equivalent, in lieu of provincial rents, purveyance, and the royal monopolies of brandy and salt, for this city, with the villages of its vicinity, is five hundred and thirty-nine thousand three hundred and sixty-one reals, or somewhat less than five thousand four hundred pounds. Now, as the whole district, or *corregimiento*, of Alicant contains, according to the government returns, thirty-three thousand and forty-five souls, the proportion of this tax is not more than sixteen reals, or about three

shillings

shillings and two pence for each inhabitant to pay.

Neither the churches, nor any of the convents, are worthy to be noticed. In the great church, indeed, I was much amused, but not with the architecture, nor yet with any of the altars; that which caught my attention was a grant from the college of cardinals, sanctioned by the archbishop and the bishop, of two thousand five hundred and eighty days indulgence to any penitent who shall say before the altar of the Virgin, *Ave Maria purissima*, and as many to all who, hearing this, shall answer, *Sin peccado Concebida*.

For the service of the great church they have ten canons, three dignitaries, and two beneficed clergy; but these are reckoned poor. The bishop's seat is at Orihuela, where the canons have a more ample provision made for them.

The commerce of Alicant is considerable. From five hundred to a thousand vessels enter annually this port, of which the major part are Catalan. In the year 1782, there entered nine hundred and sixty-one. The principal articles of export are,

Anise

Anise seeds, from three to four thousand quintals.

Almonds, from eight to ten thousand quintals.

Barrilla, from sixty to ninety thousand quintals.

Brandy, about a hundred thousand pipes.

Cumin, from two thousand to two thousand five hundred quintals.

Esparto rush, and the same in ropes and mats, the quantity uncertain.

Figs, about a thousand quintals.

Fish, uncertain quantities.

Grana sylvestre, called also vermillion, about three hundred quintals.

Lead ore, uncertain quantities.

Liquorice in root.

Lavender flowers, both to England and to Holland.

Lemon juice.

Pomegranate peel.

Raisins, from sixty to a hundred thousand quintals.

Salt, about a hundred thousand tons.

Saffron,

Silk, and

Vinegar, all uncertain in their quantities.

Wine,

Wine, about two hundred tons.

Wool, from three to four thousand quintals.

The value of our commerce with Alicant and its dependencies will appear from the following statement of the years 1784 and 1785, given to me by the English consul.

ALICANT.

[174]

ALICANT. Exports to GREAT BRITAIN, and Imports. 1784.

Ports.	Exports.	Value.
		£. s.
Alicant,	Barrilla, 7,375 bales,	40,562 10
Valencia,	Raisins, 146,560 baskets	40,304
Murviedro,	Brandy, 430 pipes,	4,300
Alicant,	Wine and Fruits,	3,800
La Matta,	Salt, 630 tons,	378
	Tonnage, 7190. by computation,	£. 89,344 10

Ports.	Imports.	Value sterling.
		£.
Alicant,	Newfoundland fish, 55,800 quintals,	34,875
Valencia,	ditto, 5,200 ditto	3,380
Denia,	ditto, 8,900 ditto,	5,785
Alicant,	Shetland lyng, 1,500 ditto	1,575
	Salted salmon, 674 tierces	1,685
	Manufactures, iron, copper, tin, &c. 2,000 woollen,	6,000
Valencia,	ditto, and ditto,	19,945
	Tonnage, 3,932.	£. 75,245

[175]

Alicant.

Exports, 1785.

		£.
Alicant,	Barrilla, 2,957 bales	21,068
Valencia, &c.	Raisins, 120,000 baskets,	39,000
Murviedro,	Brandy, 300 pipes,	3,000
Alicant,	Wine and fruits,	1,500
La Matta,	Salt, 1,600 tons	960
		£. 65,528

Tonnage, by computation, 5,712.

Imports, 1785.

		£.
Alicant,	Newfoundland fish, 45,000 quintals,	30,375
Valencia,	ditto, 15,000	10,500
Denia,	ditto, 8,900	7,700
Alicant,	Salmon, 100 tierces	275
	Shetland lyng, 1,850	1,312
	Manufactures,	1,174
	Woollen,	3,780
Valencia,	ditto and ditto	27,106
		£. 82,222

Tonnage, 3,824.

Barrilla

Barrilla is a confiderable article of commerce, and till the year 1780, was confined chiefly to this port; but fince the duties have been raifed from one hundred and fourteen maravedis and three quarters the quintal to four hundred and forty-two, being the fame that was previoufly impofed by government at Carthagena, the trade has been more equally divided. The prefent duties on the quintal of one hundred and fourteen pounds avoirdupois are as follow: royal duty, four hundred and forty-two maravedis; alcavala, thirty-five and two-thirds; brokerage and confular duty, twelve; in all about two fhillings and ten pence.

Whilft the duty on the export of Barrilla was little more than three reals the quintal, the Spanifh government exacted twenty-four for foap; in confequence of which, the oil and pot-afh were carried to Marfeilles, and made into foap, for the fervice both of Spain and of her colonies. (*v.* Campomanes, E. P. part iv. p. 249.)

Brokerage is a duty of a quarter per cent. on all commodities imported and exported, paid by the merchants to the marquis of
Paralis,

Paralis, as a compensation for the privilege of naming their own brokers; because the marquis claims the nomination under a grant from the king, to whom he had lent thirty thousand dollars, a sum equal to four thousand five hundred pounds; but to avoid the consequences of this oppressive grant, they agree to pay him the interest of a hundred thousand dollars.

Of the *Esparto rush*, M. Condom exports annually about three hundred tons from this port for Marseilles, and about fourscore cargoes, each from fifty to a hundred tons, for Genoa, Venice, and the Levant. With the raw material he is bound to send out one-third manufactured; but this part of his agreement may be, without much difficulty, eluded.

It is curious to observe the expedition and facility with which the women and children spin the esparto thread. After having soaked the rush in water, and beat it sufficiently, they, without either wheel or spindle, contrive to twist two threads at the same time; this they do by rubbing them between the palms of their hands, in the same manner as the shoemaker forms a thread upon his knee, with this difference, that one motion gives the twift to each thread, and at the fame time unites them. To keep the ends afunder, the thumb of the right hand is interpofed between them, and when that is wanted for other purpofes, the left thumb fupplies its place. Two threads being thus twifted into one, of the bignefs of a large crow-quill, forty-fix yards are fold for a quarto, or about a farthing and a fmall fraction of a farthing, and of this the materials are worth about one-fifth.

I was no lefs ftruck to fee the addrefs and difpatch with which the foft-wood turners, at Alicant, execute their work. They fit on a low ftage, above which the two poppet heads and points are raifed fix inches, and inftead of a pole and treddle they ufe a bow; to this they give motion with the right hand; the left hand holds the tool, which they guide by the conftant application of the right foot, whilft the left foot keeps the moveable poppet and point clofe up to the work. Such a pofition muft be exceedingly uneafy, till cuftom and long habit have reconciled them to it.

The

The *Grana Sylvestre* is not as yet a considerable article of commerce; it is only a few years since it was introduced. Guixona, a town about five leagues from Alicant, sends annually a number of people over all the mountains of Granada and part of Andalusia to collect it; but hitherto with no remarkable success.

Saffron of late has been in much request for a foreign market, and is collected from the vicinity of Albazete, about one hundred and twenty-five leagues from Alicant, where it is produced in considerable quantities. It is worth from fifty-five to sixty-five reals per pound, and pays on exportation, for all duties, two hundred and seven maravedis, or about fourteen pence the pound of sixteen ounces.

At Alicant the *fishery* is free from all kinds of duty; and, as a further encouragement, a tax of ten per cent. beside four hundred and eighty maravedis, by way of principal duty and millones, is laid on all foreign fish.

The dog-fish might be rendered valuable, were it not for the spirit of monopoly, and the contracted views of government.

It is good to eat, and yields about five-and-twenty pounds of oil. Beside the flesh and oil, the skin alone was usually sold for twenty reals, whilst the ports were open; but now that the exportation is prohibited, the price is sunk to eight reals, and the fishery is thereby considerably injured.

In this province, the privilege of fishing is confined to the enrolled seamen, who are about sixteen thousand.

With such a nursery for sailors in the Mediterranean, and with one similar to it in the bay of Biscay, where peculiar privileges are granted for that purpose, Spain will soon be formidable as a naval power. The Catalans already supply Alicant with pilchards, taken on the coast of Galicia; whereas formerly this city imported annually from England about fifty cargoes.

The *municipal government* of this city is in eight regidors, of which, four are noble, and four commoners; these are all considered as possessing a freehold, descending by inheritance to their children, yet not entailed upon them and therefore saleable. They have four assessors, chosen by the commons, who continue in office two years, but two are annually

ally changed. To thefe are added two fyndics, of which one, the *perfonero*, is to reprefent the grievances of the commons; but neither of thefe have votes. The ufual prefident of this court is the governor, or, in his abfence, the alcalde mayor, who refembles our recorders. In the corporation are included three phyficians and two furgeons, who have falaries.

The attendants of the court are, proctors, advocates, *efcrivanos*, and alguazils.

To keep good order in the various quarters of the city, they have *alcaldes de barrio*. Thefe formerly purchafed their office, and contrived to repay themfelves with interefl; but the prefent governor makes a new election every year, with this exception, that he continues thofe who are diftinguifhed for fidelity.

The *efcrivanos reales* are merely notaries; but the *efcrivanos del numero*, to the number of twenty-three, may be called pettyfoggers; againft thefe the governor declares a never-ceafing war; but the conteft is unequal. He attempted to reftrain their influence by the introduction of written evidence; but this attack they effectually reed. Having detected five of them in some malepractices, he sent them to prison, and at the same time gave notice, that the next offender should visit Africa. He complained to me one day in the most feeling manner, of the distress he felt in being daily witness to abuses which he was not able to correct, because these wretches can never be convicted, unless upon evidence taken by an escrivano. He lamented that, even when he knew the evidence produced was false, he was bound to give judgment agreeable to it, and could contrive no redress. Yet one point he carried, in not suffering them, as usual, to make a long and expensive process of a trifling matter.

In their turn they do all they can to harass and perplex him. The corporation having made their agreement with one contractor to supply the citizens with meat, this man caused his cattle to be driven through the city in the middle of the day. The governor remonstrated in vain. Hearing, however, repeated complaints of mischief, and seeing the people, distracted in their attention, following in crowds, as usual, wherever any thing like a bull, their favourite animal, appeared, he interpofed his authority, and abfolutely forbad the admittance of oxen after a certain hour in the morning. The contractor, on this reftraint, refufed to fupply the city, and, urged forwards by the Efcrivanos, appealed to the intendant of the province. In confequence of this appeal the governor could find no refuge, but in the direct interference of the minifter; and had his friends been lefs powerful at court, he muft have given way.

Previous to the appointment of Don Francifco Pacheco to the government of Alicant, the city fwarmed all day with beggars, and all night with proftitutes and thieves. Thefe were fed by the religious houfes, by the ecclefiaftics, and by the alms of well-difpofed yet miftaken citizens. The governor faw in a proper light both the caufe and the confequences of this abundance of unprofitable fubjects, and therefore determined to confine them; yet he knew that prejudice would run ftrong againft him. For this reafon he engaged the moft popular preachers, during Lent, to expatiate on the merit of giving to the poor,

poor, and afterwards to explain the propriety of making a diftinction in the diftribution of their alms, fo as not to offer a premium to lazinefs, prodigality, and vice.

When he had thus prepared his way, he affembled the citizens, laid his plans before them, and formed a fociety, confifting of two hundred and fifty of the firft people in the diocefe, with the bifhop, canons, and principal nobility at their head, under the denomination of "Brethren of the Poor." From thefe were elected governors and guardians for the Houfe of Mercy, and for the twelve quarters into which the city is divided, for the purpofe of taking an exact account of all the inhabitants, with their age and occupation. Every guardian, in his feveral quarter, has three affiftants to examine with him the condition of the poor, and to diftribute the relief appointed by the governors the preceding week, whether in money, in raw materials, in medicine, or in aliments, agreeable to the report which has been made to them.

In the Houfe of Mercy, children, inftructed in the moft common and therefore the moft ufeful manufactures, are trained to
induftry,

industry, and the lazy are compelled to work.

They have no other source of revenue beside the produce of their labour, and the voluntary contribution of the citizens.

This institution bears date only the 30th of June, 1786, and in May, 1787, they had expended six hundred and twenty-nine pounds for the support of about one hundred men, women, and children. These are well fed, and do little work at present; but, when they shall have been reconciled to the idea of confinement, their diet will be administered with a more sparing hand, and their labour will be rendered more productive.

They have here another institution, likely to be of extensive utility in providing for orphans, for deserted children, and for the sons of soldiers, who are burthened with numerous families. It is a military academy, in which they are taught reading, writing, and accounts, the manual exercise, and every thing needful to qualify them for serjeants. Don Francisco Pacheco had the goodness to review for me a little regiment of these, who went through all their

their evolutions, and gave their fire with wonderful addrefs. The whole number in the kingdom is two thoufand, from whom will be felected all the ferjeants for the army.

Under the fame protection, I had the happinefs of feeing a review of the artillery, with prizes diftributed to the engineers, who were moft diftinguifhed for their fkill. Much attention is paid to their education, not only at Alicant, but all over the peninfula.

The military eftablifhments of every kind appear refpectable, and mark at once wifdom and humanity in all their regulations. The foldiers are enlifted for eight years, during which they are frequently indulged with furloughs. When they have ferved fifteen years, their pay goes on conftantly increafing, and after thirty-five years, they retire with the rank of commiffioned officers, and a penfion of about twenty pounds a year.

Among the numerous objects attracting the attention of a ftranger, none was more interefting to me than the *Caftle*, with the rock on which it ftands, and that for various reafons. As an Englifhman, I was

curious

curious to examine a fortress so bravely, or rather so rashly, defended by its governor in the year 1707, more especially the chasm left by the springing of a mine, which proved fatal to General Richards, with twenty of his officers. When the Spaniards had nearly finished their work, they gave warning to the garrison; and when they had lodged in it thirteen hundred barrels of powder, they generously permitted the English general to send his engineers, who viewed the mine, with its contents. These reported, that the burthen was too great for the quantity of powder, and that the garrison was safe.

On the day appointed for the springing of this mine, people from every part of the country assembled on the opposite hill, to view the catastrophe; and notice of the fatal moment was given to the garrison. Precisely at that moment the officers, engaged in drinking, and somewhat elated by their wine, declared their resolution not to quit the battery, till they had drank two bottles more, for which they had sent a servant; but no sooner had he turned his back, than the battery, together with

with general Richards, and twenty gallant officers, mounted in the air.

By the chafm, it may be readily imagined how great muft have been the burthen; but when I had obferved the fhattered condition, and loofe-jointed nature of the rock, it became evident, that the engineers of the befieged were either ignorant or rafh in the extreme.

This fortrefs might have been battered to pieces from Mount St. Julian; but the befiegers preferred a mine. In fcrambling among the rocks, I obferved a track, very ftrongly marked, leading to a part of the fort, in which the walls are low. This being at once the fteepeft and moft rugged fide of the mountain, where I imagined no human foot-ftep had ever yet been traced, I was much furprifed to fee fo ftrong a path. It was very narrow, but well trodden; and although winding at the back of the fortrefs, it communicated with another path leading from the country to the eaftern quarter of the city.

When, on my return, I enquired very minutely into the nature and ufe of fuch a

private

private and sequestered way, this was the result of my inquiries.

The laws in many provinces of Spain being peculiarly favourable to the softer sex, if the wife complains of ill treatment from her husband, he, on her sole evidence, is confined in prison; and should she declare, on oath, that he had beaten her, the punishment would be yet more severe; he would be sent for many years to the *presidios*.

When, again, a father is displeased with the conduct of his son, if it be such as tends to bring either ruin or disgrace upon his family, the young man is sent to learn wisdom in a forced retirement.

It appears from the observations of the chief justice, Count Campomanes, in the appendix to his *Educacion popular*, that in Spain many persons of quality are shut up in prison, or sent to the *presidios*, for these and similar offences. He states, however, yet not much to the honour of the Spanish ladies, that their accusations are not always just. From him we may collect, that a great number of these fair-ones, persuaded by their cortejos, falsely charge their husbands with ill-treatment,

treatment, whenever the good men shew a disposition to be jealous.

Some young men of fashion, at the request of their fathers or their wives, are, as the governor informed me, destined to pass their tedious hours in this castle. Yet, by the connivance of the centinels, they are frequently, in the dusk of the evening, permitted to scale the walls; when, passing disguised into the city, they amuse themselves among their friends, till the company retires; after which they return by the same sequestered path to their destined habitations: and this precisely was the path which had attracted my attention.

In a conversation with the governor on the operation of a punishment long since inflicted both in France and Spain, and lately adopted in our island, that of employing criminals on public works; he perfectly agreed with me, that their labour is scarcely worth a tenth of what it costs; and assured me, that as far as his observation went, this punishment rather tended to harden them in wickedness, than to produce any reformation in their manners. He
particularly

particularly mentioned, that of the four thousand five hundred and seventy-nine convicts banished to the presidios or garrisons of Africa, the major part, on their discharge, at the expiration of their terms, returned to the eastern coast of the peninsula; and to this circumstance he attributed the prevalence of the most atrocious crimes in that part of Spain. He considered therefore the *presidios* as the worst school to which the youthful offender could be sent.

The country in the vicinity of Alicant is wild and broken; the mountains are lofty, rugged, bare, and little susceptible of cultivation; the vallies are mostly small, but remarkably fertile; the soil is sandy, with beds of clay and marle. The rock in general is calcarious; the city is partly fed by a valley to the north, and by the *Huerta*, a rich and extensive valley, to the east, at the distance of one mile, but chiefly by the vale of Murcia. The carriers bring wheat, and load back with fish.

The Huerta is watered from a vast reservoir, called *el Pantano*, constructed in the mountains, at the distance of about five leagues

leagues from Alicant. The governor had the goodness to carry me in his coach to view this artificial lake, formed between two high mountains by a wall, the dimensions of which reduced to English feet are as follow; one hundred and forty-seven high; two hundred and sixty-two wide at top, from mountain to mountain, and not more than twenty-four at bottom. The thickness of the wall is sixty-seven feet at top, and one hundred and twenty-one at bottom. It is very properly made elliptical, to sustain the lateral pressure of the water; but had the thickness of the wall been only seven feet at top, instead of sixty-seven, this would have been more than sufficient; because the area of any surface being given, the pressure of fluids on that surface is in proportion to its depth. The depth being given, it matters not whether the quantity of water be one acre, or ten thousand acres. For the same expence they might have constructed many such reservoirs, one below the other; but when we consider the age in which this was made (A. D. 1542) we are not surprised to find so much labour lost.

When

When the stream comes near the Huerta, it is separated into four by the administrator, and each proprietor of land receives, or should receive, the quantity allotted to him, in proportion to his land, paying for this the stipulated price. To prevent violence and fraud, A. D. 1739, the king, by his royal edict, established sixty-two regulations for the distribution of this water, and appointed a special court to enforce these regulations; yet notwithstanding, either through ignorance of hydrostatics in the managers, through their negligence, or through the influence of bribes, many obtain more than their just proportion, and others are left to murmur and complain. It is to be lamented, that government does not construct more pantanos. The farmers in the Huerta could dispose of five times as much as they receive at present; and were the whole interval between the mountains occupied with reservoirs, they might all be filled. This pantano, although vast, has been replenished by four hours' rain.

Independent of the produce in all kinds of grain and herbage, government derives a direct

direct revenue of near two thousand pounds a year by the distribution of this water.

The rock is a fine limestone, covering schist; and, as the country produces pines, juniper, and coscoja, in abundance, fewel for burning lime is on the spot; so that the expence of constructing reservoirs would not be great.

After having examined the pantano, I visited, on the succeeding days, the Huerta, to get acquainted with the agriculture of that rich, well planted, and well watered valley.

Going eastward from the city, having ascended gradually for about a mile, you look down upon a wide expanse of nearly thirty thousand acres, every where inclosed by lofty mountains, excepting towards the sea, and covered with oranges, lemons, figs, mulberries, almonds, cherries, apricots, peaches, nectarines, plumbs, apples, pears, pomegranates, olives, algarrobos, the more humble yet not less profitable vine, and the liquorice, with every species of grain, of leguminous plants, and of herbage for the cattle.

This vale is said to contain more than
twenty

twenty thousand persons, and I can readily believe it; for, wherever you pass, you see old and young men, women, and children innumerable, all busily employed, ploughing, sowing, reaping, treading out the grain with cattle, winnowing the corn, or conveying it to granaries, hoeing in the vineyards, distributing water to their crops, or digging their land, and preparing it for fresh productions.

When I visited this delightful vale, they had reaped their barley, and were engaged in treading it with mules. To these they added carts drawn backwards on the area, for the purpose of separating the grain, and of cutting the straw for fodder. Others were employed to wind off silk from the cones. Their reel is five feet wide, and receives six compound threads from thirty, thirty-six, or from forty-two cones, which swim in a furnace of boiling water. These threads are made to traverse on the reel, that they may not agglutinate together.

I was much pleased with the reticulated fences round most of the little farms, composed of reeds ranged in pairs, crossing each other like a lattice frame, yet so as to form, not rectangles, but lozenges or rhomboidal figures, with the reeds not interwoven, but bound together by efparto threads.

Every part of the Huerta is refreshed with water once in fifteen days during the fummer, but in winter it may go three weeks or a month unwatered. Beside the refreshing stream derived from the pantano, they have fome norias: the moft remarkable of which, belonging to Mr. Arabet, is worked by wind, and raifes the water forty feet.

The land never refts; for no fooner has it rewarded the farmer with one crop, than he begins to prepare it for another. In September he fows barley, and having reaped it about the latter end of April, or the firft week in May, he immediately puts in maize, which comes off about the middle of September. But before this ripens, he puts in fandias (the *cucurbita* of Lin.) or fome other efculent, which yields him a third crop in the courfe of the fame year. In November he fows wheat, and in June he reaps it. The produce both of wheat and barley is from fifteen to twenty-four for one, having fowed of the former nearly

two

two bushels to an acre, of the latter between three and four. Flax is put into the ground about September, or the beginning of October, and comes off in May; but hemp, which is sowed in April, continues on the land till August. These, with cucumbers, melons, *garbanzos (cicer* arietinum), peas, French beans, lettuce, alfalfa (*Medicago* sativa), form a rich variety of crops, which, cherished by a bright sun and fed by abundant streams from the pantano, prove a never-failing source of plenty.

In the spring they abound with oranges and lemons; in summer they have plumbs, cherries, figs, apricots, and nectarines; in autumn they gather grapes; and in winter a rich variety of fruits supplies their tables. Thus Ceres and Pomona appear to be engaged in a never-ceasing contest which shall most contribute to the wealth and prosperity of this favoured valley.

One of the most valuable productions of this country is the barilla. For this they plough their land four or five times, dung it well, and then, having turned the earth twice more, they make it smooth with boards

boards instead of harrows, and sow their seed in the months of January and February, waiting always for wet weather.

When the plant is about the bigness of a shilling, they clear off all the weeds, and in September they collect the crop into heaps of about six feet high. Of these they burn fifty in one hole, stirring well the broth with sticks; then, protecting it from rain, at the expiration of eight or ten days, the stone will be cold enough to be removed.

Beside the barilla *(salsola soda* of Linnæus) this vicinity produces many other species, which, by combustion, yield the pot-ash. These are,

1st, Aguaful, or *mesembryanthemum*.

2d, Salicor, *Salicornea Europæa*, of two species, one annual in swamps, the other perennial in dry and stony places.

3d, Barilla punchosa soda colorada, *salsola kali*. This gives few ashes, and little salt.

4th, Sosa prima, *chenopodium maritimum*. This plant is the most common, and is to be found all along the coast.

5th, Sosa blanca, *chenopodium album*.

6th,

6th, Sofa gorda, *falfola vermicularis*.
7th, Sofa leñofa, *falfola rofacea*.
8th, Hyerba de la plata, *mefembryanthemum* cryſt.

Of thefe the falfola kali, the falicornia, and the chenopodia, are found in England; but they do not produce a fufficient quantity of falt to make the cultivation of them profitable.

The rapid progrefs of vegetation in warm climates fills the inhabitants of more northern regions with aftonifhment. Having one day expreffed my furprife on this fubject to the governor, he carried me in the evening to the garden of Don Lorenzo Mabile, at a little diftance from the city, where we wandered about under the fhade of trees, which four years before had no exiſtence but as flips, as feedlings, or as fuckers. We obſerved three hundred fig-trees, and three thouſand five hundred vines, loaded with fruit; and he already drinks in his family the wine of his own vineyard. Befide thefe, he has collected together innumerable pomegranates, apricots, apples, pears, plumbs, mulberries, oranges, lemons, algarrobos, and azaroles *(cratægus)*

(cratægus), which by their luxuriant growth seem to have been planted at least twenty years.

From this vineyard he made last year three tons and an half of wine, each vine on the average yielding one quart.

The whole produce of Alicant is about four thousand tons.

For the Fontillon wine, the grapes are gathered, picked from the stalks, and exposed on elevated wicker frames for the space of fifteen days to the influence of the sun and wind, in order to evaporate the superfluous moisture, after which they are submitted to the press.

Among the natural curiosities in the vicinity of Alicant, the most remarkable are the baths of Buzot. Having heard a description of them from a physician, I resolved to visit them before I left the city, and, for that purpose, I formed a party on the 31st of May. Early in the morning we mounted our horses, and, having passed through the Huerta, we ascended suddenly twelve or fourteen feet to a plain, upon a higher level, called the *Campillo*, which, like the Huerta, is watered by the pantano.

After

After having traversed this well cultivated and fertile plain, we began to climb the hills, and, at the distance of four leagues from Alicant, near to the village of *las Aguas*, we arrived at the romantic spot, where the warm springs break out.

This country is broken by high mountains, of which the most remarkable are the Buchampana, the Sierra Gitana, and the Cabezo, so called by contraction from *cabeza de auro*, or head of gold. The Sierra Gitana derives its appellation from the gipsies. This elevated chain, exposed to every storm, is far from being a desirable abode, because the lightning breaks upon it with more than common violence, and the thunder is reverberated by its innumerable rocks. These rocks are calcarious, and discover fossil shells. Here I found some marmor metalicum, or ponderous earth, with gypsum or calcarious earth, each saturated with vitriolic acid; and in many places I picked up iron ore with hæmatites.

On the southern declivity, near to the base of these lofty mountains, four copious mineral springs break forth, two of them near together, the others more remote. Their temperature is about one hundred and

four

four degrees of Fahrenheit's thermometer. They have evidently the chalybeate taste, deposit a sediment of yellow ochre, and, upon evaporation, Glauber's and sea salt are found cryftallized in it. Two or three small tumblers filled from any of these springs prove speedily and pleasantly cathartic.

This part of the country is frequently shaken by strong earthquakes.

I had here an opportunity to examine the natural history of the *grana kermes*. It is found on the cofcoja, or *quercus coccifera* of Linnæus, here growing to the height of from twelve inches to two feet. The grana appear on the stems or small branches, some near the bottom of the plant, but mostly on the upper branches, yet always protected by the leaves, and fixed to the stem by a gluten, which both to the sight and to the touch resembles thin white leather, spread over the stem and covering, like the cup or calix of the acorn, a segment of the grana. Upon a more minute investigation, I traced the agglutinating coat through a small foramen into the grana, from whence it had proceeded, and where it spread, like the placenta, on the internal surface.

*

The

The grana were of various sizes, from an eighth to a quarter of an inch in diameter, perfectly spherical, and covered with a white powder, which being rubbed off, the surface appeared red, smooth, and polished. Upon the same stem I found the grana in three stages. In the first I discovered only tough membranes filled with a red juice resembling blood, but on paper leaving a stain as bright and beautiful as the best carmine. In the second stage there appeared, under the first coat or pellicle, a thin tough membrane inclosing the eggs, now most minute, and scarcely to be distinguished without the assistance of a convex lens. Between this membrane and the pellicle was the same red liquor, but less in quantity than was contained in the former stage. By a careful dissection I took off the pellicle, which was evidently separated from the inner membrane by what seemed to be the viscera and blood-vessels, but near to the foramen these two coats adhered closely together.

The interior membrane is thin, white, and tough, with a lunar septum, forming the ovary, which at first is very small, and scarcely discernible, but progressively enlarges,

larges, till in the third stage it occupies the whole space, when the tincturing juice disappears, and only eggs are to be seen, to the number of fifteen hundred or two thousand.

It is clear to me that the grana derives no kind of nourishment from the plant on which it is fixed; and from its position I am inclined to think, that the little animal chooses the quercus coccifera, which in its prickly leaf resembles the holly, only for the sake of shelter and protection from birds.

I put some of the grana into a coffee-cup on the thirty-first of May, and, June the twelfth, I discovered a multitude of animalculæ, of a bright red colour, exceedingly minute, running about the cup with astonishing rapidity, but for short intervals. A friend put some grana into a snuff-box, where he soon forgot them; but when, at the distance of a few weeks, he had occasion to resume his box; he found the top covered internally with dew, and a multitude of winged insects, all dead, adhering to it.

Before

Before my excursion to Buzot, some peasants of Las Aguas had spread themselves on the adjacent mountains, where they collected more than four arrobas, or one hundred weight of grana, which they had sold in Alicant for fifteen reals, or about three shillings a pound.

Beside the grana kermes, I observed on the coscoja many large red excrescences; and of these, two species are distinguished, the one formed on the leaf, the other on the stems of the amentaceous flowers. The former appears in the middle of the leaf, on both its surfaces, and is at first of a green colour; but as it swells, it becomes of a bright red, and occupies the whole leaf, with this exception, that in some a narrow margin of the leaf remains. The latter are longer than the former, and where they are found, the stems of the amenta are considerably larger than the rest; yet the florets, which appear on the surface of these excrescences, are not to appearance affected by them. These morbid tumors have many perforations, communicating with little cells, which contain each a small white grub. The
cell

cell is formed by a strong membrane, but the substance of the tumor is spongy. In the excrescence on the leaf I could not discover any nidus, although I have no doubt that these, like the former, were occasioned by the ichneumon fly, and that each of them contained an egg.

I might here proceed to give at large the natural history of the locust; but this task having been so well performed by the judicious Bowles, I shall be exceedingly brief upon the subject. These voracious insects commit the greatest devastations in the south of Spain; and this proceeds, not merely from the warmth of the climate, but from want of cultivation, because the females never deposit their eggs in arable land, but always in the deserts. For this reason Galicia, where agriculture prevails, is little infested with the locust.

Adanson, in his voyage to Senegal, has given us a striking picture of the desolation occasioned by a cloud of locusts which darkened the sun, and extending many leagues, in the space of a few hours laid waste the country, devouring fruits, and leaves, and herbage, the bark of trees, and
even

even the dried reeds with which the huts were thatched.

Of the locust tribe, Linnæus reckons twenty species. Those I have observed in Spain are the *Grylli Italici*, distinguished by the redness of their wings. Their jaw bones are strong, and dented like a saw. Their head bears a striking resemblance to that of the horse, and this similitude has been remarked in the whole genus. The sound of their wings is said to be like the noise of distant chariots.

They are not always considered as a plague, being commonly seen only in the forests; but when the season has been peculiarly favourable for their propagation; when these rapacious insects darken the air; when their assembled hosts fall upon the rich pastures; when they rob the vines and olives of their foliage; when they devour the corn; when they enter the houses, and lay waste every thing before them, they are then universally regarded as the scourge of heaven. As such they were considered, when, for four successive years, from 1754 to 1757, they ravaged all the southern provinces of Spain and Portugal.

The description of this gloomy scene, at least of one similar to it, which a prophet has given us, is scarcely to be equalled for beauty and poetic fire. He calls upon the people to lament, because a nation, strong and without number, whose teeth are the teeth of lions, had suddenly invaded them. Then, turning to the heralds,

" Blow ye the trumpet in Zion, and sound an alarm in my holy mountain. Let all the inhabitants of the land tremble, for the day of the Lord cometh, for it is nigh at hand: a day of darkness, and of gloominess; a day of clouds and thick darkness; as the morning spread upon the mountains, a people great and strong: there hath not been ever the like, neither shall be any more after it, even to the years of many generations. A fire devoureth before them, and behind them a flame burneth. The land is as the garden of Eden before them, and behind them a desolate wilderness, yea, and nothing shall escape them. The appearance of them is as the appearance of horses; and as horsemen, so shall they run. Like

Like the noise of chariots on the tops of mountains shall they leap; like the noise of a flame of fire that devoureth the stubble; as a strong nation set in battle array. Before their face the people shall be much pained: all faces shall gather blackness. They shall run like mighty men; they shall climb the wall like men of war; and they shall march every one on his way, and they shall not break their ranks; neither shall one thrust another; they shall walk every one in his path, and when they fall upon the sword they shall not be wounded. They shall run to and fro in the city; they shall run upon the wall; they shall climb up upon the houses; they shall enter in at the windows like a thief. The earth shall quake before them; the heavens shall tremble; the sun and the moon shall be dark, and the stars shall withdraw their shining. And the Lord shall utter his voice before his army, for his camp is very great; for he is strong that executeth his word; for the day of the Lord is great and very terrible, and who can abide it."

JOEL, cap. ii. 1—11.

Their usual resort is in the forests, and in deserts, where they may safely lodge their eggs without fear of having them disturbed. The female being impregnated, the male hastens to the river, and is drowned in the stream. The female then deposits her eggs in the nearest uncultivated spot, and protects them from the rain by a covering of glue. Having finished this work, exhausted with fatigue, she drinks and dies.

The eggs are hatched in March, in April, or in May, according to the situation and the season. When hatched, the assembled tribes continue together for about three weeks, till their legs, and teeth, and wings have acquired strength, after which they disperse themselves over the neighbouring country, and devour every kind of vegetable.

When the provincial governors are informed, in spring, that locusts have been seen, they collect the soldiers and the peasants, divide them into companies, and surround the district. Every man is furnished with a long broom, with which he strikes the ground, and thus drives the young locusts

towards

towards a common centre, where a vaſt excavation, with a quantity of bruſh-wood, is prepared for their reception, and where the flame deſtroys them.

A. D. 1780, three thouſand men were thus employed at Zamora for three weeks; and it was reckoned that the quantity collected exceeded ten thouſand buſhels.

A botaniſt, in the vicinity of Alicant, may have in that purſuit alone, full employment for his time. On the mountains he will find the eſparto ruſh, junipers, pines, the cofcoja, roſemary, thyme, mint, ſage, lavender, many ſpecies of the ciſtus, and a vaſt variety of plants too tedious to be enumerated. Thoſe which ſtruck my attention moſt were the ciſtus, the caper, with its beautiful white petals and purple ſtamina, and the Nerium Oleander.

Without going twenty miles from the city, you meet with every climate of the temperate zone, either by aſcending the mountains, or keeping near the ſea. From this circumſtance, the botaniſt derives the greateſt advantages in the proſecution of his favourite amuſement.

My principal object was the foſſil kingdom.

dom. With a view to that I examined mount St. Julian near the city. The summit is calcarious freeftone, with cockles, beaked oyfters, and fome other bivalves. Under this lies a ftratum of gypfum, charged with fragments of flate, then calcarious rock, with foffil fhells. After this, near the level of the fea, is a ftratum of fhells, divided into an upper layer of fmall fragments; and one inferior to this, compofed entirely of fhells, moftly perfect, and cemented together by broken fragments, yet unmixed with heterogeneous matter. Beneath this comes a ftratum of pudding rock, fome loofe bowlder ftones, all calcarious, and a few fhells. This ftratum is near to the waters edge.

The rock, on which ftands the caftle of Alicant, is calcarious, and abounds in fragments of foffil fhells; but the Sierra to the north, beyond the vallies, evidently appears to be compofed of fchift.

I was much furprifed to find in Mount St. Julian fuch difcordance in the fhells depofited in the rock at different levels. Near the fummit, the foffil bodies are bedded in the rock, and petrified themfelves;

but

but near the level of the sea they are loose, and appear scarcely changed; the former, as we have seen, are cockles, oysters, and some other bivalves; the latter are, the areæ, cunei, buccina, cassides, cylindri, murices, cochleæ, and pectenoides of Da Costa, of which species not one appears upon a higher level. I was the more forcibly struck with this difference, at different levels, from a recollection of the Hampshire fossils picked up under Hordwell Cliffs by Mr. Brander, and described by Dr. Solander, compared with those to be found on the limestone hills in the vicinity of Yeovil, of Sherborn, and in Marston Moor; for in these may be observed precisely the same discordance.

Such facts, wherever they occur, as they may hereafter assist us in acquiring a more perfect knowledge of the changes which have in remote periods, happened to the earth, should be carefully recorded.

About two leagues from Alicant is a mountain, called Alcoray, in which the rock is calcarious, charged with extraneous fossils. Here they have discovered cinnabar

nabar and red gypsum, which is perhaps coloured by the cinnabar.

I shall content myself for the present with having recorded facts: hereafter, when occasion offers, I shall refer to them again, and perhaps raise some theory upon them, if at least, in the mean time, a gentleman, who is infinitely better qualified to treat this subject, should not be prevailed upon to communicate his thoughts. Should he indulge the public with his Observations on the Deluge, we shall then be happy in possessing a complete register of facts, and may hope for some consistent theory, such as will stand the test of ages, and be confirmed by every subsequent discovery.

Of *diseases*, the one most prevalent in this part of Spain is the intermittent fever, arising here, not from marsh miasmata, but from the quantity of melons and *sandias*, (a species of *cucurbita*), which the peasants eat, and from their hard labour, when exposed to a scorching sun. For this, in the beginning of the disorder, the patient is bled four times, and drinks lemonade; after which, in seven, or at most in fourteen days, unless death should intervene, he

usually

usually recovers. Should any visceral obstructions indicate, in the opinion of the faculty, such treatment, the Peruvian bark is administered in small quantities, and is said to complete the cure. This account I have from a physician of the royal hospital, who favoured me with a minute relation of his theory and practice in this disease.

It is happy for the people that they have another source of hope, under the various diseases incident to the human frame, beside the skill of their physicians, a source of hope that never fails them at any season of distress. Thus, for instance, St. Anthony, the abbot, secures his votaries from fire; and St. Anthony of Padua delivers them from water; S. Barbara is the refuge of the timid in times of thunder and of war; St. Blass cures disorders of the throat; S. Lucia heals all diseases of the eyes; St. Nicholas is the patron of young women, who desire to be married; St. Ramon is their powerful protector during pregnancy; and St. Lazaro assists them when in labour; S. Polonia preserves the teeth; St. Domingo cures the fever; and St. Roque is the saint invoked

invoked under apprehenfions of the plague. And thus in all difeafes, under every preffure of affliction, fome faint is acceffible by prayer, whofe peculiar province it is to relieve the object of diftrefs.

In feafons of general calamity, when, not individuals, but the community is threatened with peftilence or famine; when the ufual patrons are either deaf to their prayers, or have no power to affift them; public proceffions are appointed, and the *SSma faz* is exhibited to view. This moft facred relick, like its rival the *SSmo fudario*, preferved among other valuable remains in the cathedral of Oviedo, is the exact reprefentation of the Redeemer's face, impreffed on the handkerchief of Santa Veronica, of which three only were produced.

A learned jefuit has favoured the world with the authentic hiftory of this ineftimable treafure. Of the three impreffions, one is at Rome, a fecond is acknowledged to be at Jaen, and the third was for a time depofited at Jerufalem. This, at a feafon when perfecution raged, was fent to the king of Cyprus, and from that ill-fated ifland it fought refuge in a private chapel belonging

ing to the Pope. Here it rested for a time; but having been sent to Venice, where the plague was raging, it acquired such reputation, that the Venetians were determined to retain it for ever in their city. The Pope reclaimed his treasure, and a cardinal was sent to conduct it back to Rome; but in the mean time his holiness having by death caused a vacancy in the papal throne, the good cardinal made a present of his charge to a chaplain, who was appointed curate of San Juan, in the Huerta of Alicant, and thither it travelled with him.

This man, little knowing the treasure he possessed, threw it carelessly into a chest, and covered it with all his stock of clothes; but to his astonishment, when he opened the chest, the sacred image was at the top. Thinking, however, that his servants might have placed it there, he again thrust it to the bottom. This happened thrice, and a third time, to his confusion, he found it on the surface. This wonderful event proved the revival of its fame; and from that period the succession of miracles wrought by its superior energy has been unremitted.

It

It happens unfortunately for this ineftimable relick, that the face is much fmaller than natural; whereas thofe of Jaen, of Oviedo, and of Rome, are all of the proper fize. But then it is remarked by the learned jefuit, that, according to the teftimony of the reverend monks who perform the facred offices in the convent of Santa Clara, where it is preferved, the face does not always appear of the fame fize, being fometimes indeed diminutive, but at other times vifibly as large as thofe of Jaen and of Rome.

Of late there have been no authentic records of its averting either peftilence or famine; but in the year 1489, after a long drought, being carried in proceffion, refrefhing fhowers immediately fucceeded, and from that time it has been confidered as the richeft treafure of the *Huerta*.

I am not fufficiently acquainted with the topography of the ancient city, with its chronology, or with the geography of the furrounding country, to fit in judgment on the hiftory of this learned jefuit, who ftates, that when, in the year 1489, the curate of S. Juan, in the Huerta, affifted by two Francifcan

cifcan friars, was carrying the *SSma faz* to Alicant, he paffed a little ravin, called Lloxia, and made a ftand on a rifing ground beyond it: but I am inclined to fufpect that he did not recollect the fituation of the city at the time to which his miracle refers. I leave this matter, therefore, to be difcuffed by others.

Alicant ftood formerly about a league further to the eaftward than at prefent, on the other fide of Mount S. Julian, not far from the cape *de la Huerta*, and the modern city, fo late as the year 1519, confifted merely of fix cottages; but in three and forty years fubfequent to that period, one thoufand families had taken refuge in it from the ravages of the Algerines.

All the ancient houfes in the Huerta, by their lofty and ftrong towers, evidently fhew how much were dreaded the depredations of thofe pirates; and the vaft increafe of Alicant proves the peace and fecurity its citizens have enjoyed under the protection of its caftle. Even fo late as the year 1776, the Algerines invaded, like a flight of locufts, all the fea coaft of Catalonia, Valencia, and Granada, but they were foon repulfed.

I had

I had the curiosity to ask Don Francisco Pacheco his opinion respecting the failure of the Spanish expedition against Algiers. He was present on that memorable day, and being both high in command, and a confidential friend of General O'Reilly, he was competent to form a judgment of his conduct. The armament consisted of twenty thousand men, with a strong fleet to cover them; but the boats were capable of receiving only eight thousand men. The first division, therefore, was ordered to form upon the strand, and to rest upon their arms till the whole force should be disembarked, because the design of the general was to move in columns, and to take possession of a mountain which commanded the city of Algiers. This division made good its landing, and met with nothing to molest them; but the commanding officer, seeing the Moors assembled to oppose him, yet not in force, impatient to gather laurels, instead of halting agreeable to orders, cried out, *a ellas mishijos, at them my sons*, and rushed forward to the attack. The enemy retired, and he continued to pursue them till his men were harassed, and thrown into confusion

fusion by multitudes who lay hid behind camels, rocks, and bushes.

The second division hastened to support the first, but it was now too late, and the confusion becoming general, the commander in chief was obliged to order a retreat. This he conducted with such skill, that, embarking his troops in sight of more than a hundred and fifty thousand Moors, he saved his artillery, and lost only four hundred and sixty men; a trifling loss, when it is considered that they had been skirmishing fourteen hours without intermission.

Had it not been for the rashness of the officer who had the command of the troops first landed, the city must in three days have been reduced to ashes.

On the testimony of such a witness, I can neither doubt these facts, nor the conclusion which he drew from them; for of all the persons of rank, whom I had the honour to approach, I no where saw his equal for good sense, for firmness, and for probity.

The highest gratification attached to travelling is the pleasure of conversing with distinguished characters. This pleasure

sure is so great, that had I met with one only such as the governor of Alicant, I should have been well rewarded for the fatigues of a long and of a tedious journey. I think I never saw a brighter model of perfection. Calm and recollected, he appears always to command himself; bold and intrepid, he makes the most obstinate to obey; yet so mild and gentle are his manners, and so much benevolence appears in his words and in his actions, that all but those who violate the laws, feel inclined to cultivate his friendship. As a knight of Malta, he has a rich commandery in a delightful situation, where he might enjoy every gratification which this world can give, excepting that of being extensively useful to mankind. For this reason he chooses rather to continue in his government of Alicant, where he meets with contradictions and vexations at every step he takes, either for the improvement of the city, or for the establishment of a regular police. His perseverance, however, will surmount all difficulties, and the latest posterity will bless the remembrance of his name.

In viewing such a character, one cannot help lamenting that he should be a knight of Malta, and therefore a stranger to domestic comfort. Although a knight of Malta, he appears not insensible to the charms of beauty; for speaking one day of the Andalusian women, of their persons, their gracefulness, and their animation, he remarked with feeling, that such superlative beauty was sufficient to turn a wise man's head. I quit with much regret the contemplation of so amiable a character.

The *weights* and *measures* of Alicant differ from those of other provinces.

The *quintal* is four arrobas of twenty-four pounds each, and the pound is of eighteen ounces Spanish, or nineteen English; consequently the quintal is two pounds heavier than our hundred weight.

The *vara*, of four palms, is very nearly equal to the English yard.

The *cantaro* is four azumbres, or thirty medias, and is equal to three gallons. It is used for liquids.

The *cahiz* contains twelve barchillas, or forty-eight celemines, and is equal to seven bushels and a half.

Eight *quartos* are equal to nine farthings.

The price of *Provisions*.

Bread—four quartos for sixteen ounces.

Beef—ten quartos the pound of eighteen ounces now, but twelve years ago it was only six quartos and a half.

Mutton—sixteen quartos and a half now, but at that period thirteen.

Veal—seventeen quartos.

Pork—eighteen quartos.

Fresh fish—commonly eight quartos.

Oil—nineteen quartos the pound, but by the arroba thirty-three reals.

A fowl, big or little, is fifteen quartos.

Salt is twenty-eight reals the fanega, or hundred weight, at the Alfori, or the king's store; where an administrator, a fiel medidor or meter, an escrivano, and a visitador or supervisor, give attendance.

The contract for provisions is made for six years.

JOURNEY

JOURNEY

FROM

ALICANT TO VALENCIA.

JUNE 6th, I left Alicant. In the vale, the only thing which ſtruck my attention was one of the Moorifh fountains; but as we aſcended to a higher level, I became intereſted in the ſtrata. Here I ſaw what I had before conjectured, that theſe high mountains are compoſed principally of ſchiſt, and that the ſchiſt is capped with limeſtone; yet ſome of the ſtrata are of gypſum. From theſe heights we deſcended to the rich valley of Montfort, which is watered by copious ſtreams, and apparently well cultivated. The ſoil is light, and in their ploughs they employ one mule, yet the land produces abundantly, oil, wine, figs, grain of every species, and barilla. The tomato and the capsicum seem to be in great requeſt. Montfort is four leagues from Alicant.

After dinner, we proceeded five leagues more to Villena. The way chiefly paſſes through a rude uncultivated country, between barren mountains of gypſum, which are altogether deſerted, and fit only for monumental croſſes. In a ravin, I obſerved a little ſtream, flowing over a bed of ſelenite, whoſe margin is covered with ſea-ſalt. Having paſſed the mountains, we entered the fertile vale of Elda, where vines, almonds, figs, and olives, with wheat, maize, barley, and alfalfa, cover the wide expanſe. In the vineyards they were ploughing with two mules, but in the open field they uſe a ſingle aſs. On the left, between Elda and Villena, is *Sax*, a village of two thouſand ſouls, in a moſt romantic ſituation, at the foot of a ſteep and rugged mountain, on the ſummit of which is an old caſtle looking perpendicularly down upon the village, with its adjacent plain. Having croſ-
fed

fed this plain, we travelled between high rocks and mountains to Villena.

Villena is a confiderable city, placed at the termination of a fierra, called S. Chriftobal. It contains two thoufand five hundred families, divided into two parifhes, with two convents for men, one for women, a congregation of S. Philip Neri, a palace for the marquis its proprietor, and feveral other confiderable edifices. On the adjoining mountain is a very ancient caftle, formerly a place of ftrength, but commanded by a more elevated mountain.

In this city are eftablifhed manufactures of foap and linen, with many diftilleries for brandy.

The public walks are very pleafant, and well laid out; the fountains fend out copious ftreams, and together form a rivulet by which the plain is watered.

Thus plentifully watered, this extenfive plain produces wheat, barley, oats, rye, maize, leeks, onions, parfnips, alfalfa, hemp, vines, olives, figs, and mulberries.

Near the city is a lake of falt, two leagues in circumference; and at the diftance of four leagues, a hill, compofed of rock-falt, is covered with gypfum.

Provifions on the whole are reafonable: beef being fold for fix quartos, or fomething under feven farthings, a pound of fixteen ounces; but mutton is worth fourteen quartos, or nearly four pence.

In the *pofada* I obferved, that the windows have no kind of faftening; from which I collect, either that remarkable fimplicity prevails, or that a watchful police reftrains the fallies of intemperance, with the depredations of confequent diftrefs.

All the rocks in this vicinity are limeftone.

June 7th, at five in the morning, we proceeded on our journey over the plain to Fuente la Higuera, leaving *Almanza* to the left, at the diftance of near a league.

Bifhop Burnet is miftaken in the account he has given us of the famous battle of Almanza. The fact was fimply this: the duke of Berwick, anxious to bring on a decifive action, fent two fpies into lord Galway's camp, under pretence of being deferters, with a report that the duke of Orleans was conducting from France a reinforcement

inforcement of twelve thousand men; that in two days he was expected to arrive, when the two dukes, with their united forces, would compel the English to engage. Lord Galway fell into the snare, raised the siege of Villena, marched his army, April 14th, three long leagues, and in the middle of the day, with his fainting troops, attacked the duke of Berwick, who was calmly waiting to receive him. The event was such as might be well expected; for, by this stratagem, the duke put the crown on the head of Philip, and, by his valour, he preserved it there.

The day after this engagement, the duke of Orleans, with only fourteen attendants, joined the victorious army.

Fuente la Higuera, a village of between two and three thousand inhabitants, is built on a rock, surrounded by high mountains of lime-stone, and looks down upon a fertile valley. It is not well cultivated; yet such is the richness of the soil, that all the crops are good, and the trees are most luxuriant in their growth. Were it well watered, it would certainly be more productive.

This village belongs, with many in its vicinity,

vicinity, to the marquis de dos Aguas, who names the magiftrates.

When we left Fuente la Higuera, we joined company with five men, who had the charge of fix horfes, all loaded with dollars, and bound for France. As foon as we had defcended to the plain, every man croffed himfelf, difcharged his mufket, then loaded his piece afrefh, and flung it by his horfe's fide.

From this delightful plain we foon entered a contracted valley, fhut in by lime-ftone rocks, where the profpect changes at every ftep. All the level fpots are covered with wheat, barley, oats, or maize; the higher lands are allotted to olives, figs, or vines; and the rugged moors, unfufceptible of culture, are abandoned to rofemary, thyme, mint, lavender, and the lovely oleander, whilft lofty pines vary the fcene, and crown the moft elevated rocks. The road is lately finifhed; it is rounded, well ftoned, and perfectly ftraight. As we advance, the valley widens, and we admire groves of algarrobos, with olives and extenfive vineyards.

On the left hand we look up to the defolated

solated convent and castle of *Montesa*, built for the military order of that name, A. D. 1319, by D. Jayme 2d, and ruined by an earthquake, 23d March, 1748.

This country is frequently convulsed; and it is remarkable that, previous to the shock, the wells are all affected, rising and falling suddenly between wide extremes.

At the end of every league we see a neat cottage with its garden, the habitation of the *guardia de camino*, whose office it is to defend the traveller, and to mend the road. For this purpose he is furnished with proper arms and tools; and for his pay he receives five reals, or one shilling, daily.

About seven in the evening we arrived at *Roblar*, and went to the *posada del rey*, a modern edifice, built by the king, well furnished, and administered on his majesty's account. The beds are excellent, with paillasse, mattress, and fine linen. In the morning, when I drank my chocolate, they brought me a beautiful china cup and saucer, made at the royal manufactory of the *buen retiro*, in imitation of the French. The price of every thing is fixed, and the adminiſtrator is remarkably attentive to his gueſts. It is, without exception, the moſt comfortable inn I have met with in Spain. They have fourteen bed-rooms, a kitchen for the common carriers, a ſpacious coach-houſe, and ſtabling for three hundred and thirty horſes, mules, and aſſes.

From hence we look up to Xativa, or Sætabis, now called San Felipe, a city containing about ten thouſand ſouls, with eight convents for monks, and two for nuns. This circumſtance beſpeaks the richneſs and beauty of the country. Indeed no valley can be more fertile than this extenſive plain; the whole appears to be a garden, covered with the moſt luxuriant herbage, bearing three crops in the year, and yielding wheat, barley, rye, beans, peas, rice, maize, oil, wine, and ſilk, in great abundance.

Xativa had the honour of giving birth to Joſeph Ribera, better known by the name of Eſpañoleto.

On theſe mountains we ſee limeſtone, marble, alabaſter, and gypſum, of various colours. In the former, foſſil-ſhells are found.

When we leave this plain, we again traverse the mountains, where we have occasion to admire the patience and perseverance of the Spanish character. They are now making a new road, and seem resolved to keep it on a level, notwithstanding the inequality of the ground over which they are to pass, not turning either to the right hand or to the left. If they meet with a deep ravin, they fill it up; if with a hill, they cut through it. I observed them in one place, rather than deviate a little from a right line, cutting a wide passage through a limestone rock for a considerable way, to the depth of more than fifty feet. Their ambition scorns all bounds; and, by their strenuous exertions, they seem determined to remove every obstacle which can impede them in their progress to absolute perfection.

From the summit of these mountains we have an extensive prospect, and look down upon the rich valley of Valencia.

Here I picked up some beautiful red gypsum. Several veins of cinnabar have been discovered in this neighbourhood in calcarious rock; but I do not mean to assert fert that the gypfum is coloured by this mineral.

About four in the evening we arrived at Valencia, having travelled, in three days, twenty-feven leagues, or about a hundred miles.

VALENCIA.

VALENCIA.

THE situation of Valencia is delightful, and the country round it is a perfect garden, watered by the Guadalaviar, on the banks of which the city stands. It is divided into fourteen parishes, including the cathedral, and is said to contain a hundred thousand souls. On the average of two years, A. D. 1782 and 1786, the marriages were six hundred and eighty-one; the births, two thousand six hundred; the burials, two thousand five hundred and twenty-five. The city is evidently flourishing; and, were we to judge by the returns to government, we should be inclined to think the progress, in respect of population, since the commencement of the present century, had been rapid. In the whole province, A. D. 1718, when the equivalent

was

was settled, they reckoned sixty-three thousand seven hundred and seventy families, and two hundred and fifty-five thousand souls. A. D. 1761, these amounted, when numbered for the quintas, or levies for the army, to one hundred and fifty-one thousand one hundred and twenty-eight famlies, and six hundred and four thousand six hundred and twelve souls. A. D. 1768, Count d'Aranda obtained an account from the bishops of one hundred and seventy nine thousand two hundred and twenty-one families, and seven hundred and sixteen thousand eight hundred and eighty-six souls; and now, by the last returns, we may calculate them at one hundred and ninety-two thousand nine hundred and seventy families, because we find seven hundred and seventy-one thousand eight hundred and eighty-one souls. In this province they reckon only four persons to one vecino or master of a family.

In a city like Valencia we naturally expect to see many convents: they are indeed numerous, being no fewer than forty-four, nearly divided between the monks and nuns.

nuns. Beside these, we find ten churches, belonging to congregations, colleges, and hospitals.

The streets are narrow, crooked, and not paved; yet they are clean, and therefore healthy.

The principal buildings are, the cathedral, the convents, and the university; of which the former, without comparison, is the most worthy of attention. It is of Grecian architecture; light, elegant, and highly finished, more especially in the dome, and in six of the larger chapels. Altogether I never saw a more pleasing structure.

Near to the entrance, the first chapel to the right, opposite to the high altar, is dedicated to S. Sebastian. This contains a good picture of the saint, by Pedro Orrhente of Murcia. Next to this, when you have passed the entrance to the chapterhouse, is the chapel *de la comunion*, with its cupola and three altars. Similar to this are the chapels of S. Francis of Borja, of S. Pasqual, and of S. Thomas. The former of these is elegantly fitted up by the countess tefs of Peñafiel, who, as dutchefs of Gandia, owes peculiar reverence to S. Francis, once the lord of Gandia, and now its patron. The crofs iles have each four altars, and maffive marble pillars. Behind the great altar, eight little chapels, decorated with marble columns, contribute much to the beauty of this edifice. To the north, the church is fitted up in much the fame manner as we defcribed it in the fouth; and round the choir, in twelve receffes, are twelve altars, making altogether fifty-four altars, at moft of which incenfe is daily offered.

The great altar, thirty feet high by eighteen wide, is filver; and the image of the Bleffed Virgin, fix feet high, is of the fame precious metal: the workmanfhip of both is admirable. On the altar, in eight feveral compartiments, are reprefented, in bold relief, as many facred fubjects, executed by the beft mafters who lived at the clofe of the fifteenth century. Thefe are protected by folding doors, of greater value for their paintings than the altar itfelf for the filver it contains. The fubjects are twelve; fix on the outfide, and as many

on

on the infide, the production of Francis Neapoli, and of Paul Aregio.

In the facrifty, I faw a maffive fepulchre of filver gilt, defigned for the reception of the hoft on good Friday; a magnificent throne and canopy of filver, for Eafter Sunday; and, of the fame metal, two cuftodias, one with Corinthian columns, and images of the two patron faints; the other, twelve feet high, with a gold border, innumerable gems, and a little image of S. Michael the archangel, compofed entirely of brilliants. This was added to the treafures of the church in the year 1452.

All the beft pictures are difpofed of in the facrifty and chapter-houfe. Thofe by the canon Victoria, and by Vergara, are excellent; but the moft beautiful, and little inferior to Raphael's, are many by Juanes; more efpecially his Holy Family, in the chapter-houfe, and his Ecce Homo, in a chapel of that name.

Among the relics, thofe held in the higheft eftimation are, many thorns of the Redeemer's crown; the curious cup in which he drank at his laft fupper; and a
wretched

wretched picture of the Blessed Virgin, painted by S. Luke.

The revenues of this church are considerable. The archbishop has one hundred and sixty thousand pesos, or twenty-four thousand pounds a year; seven dignitaries have each from eight to fourteen hundred pesos; twenty-six canons, ten lecturers, a master of ceremonies, chantors, assistants, &c. to the number of three hundred, are all well provided for.

Whenever the nation shall be reduced to the necessity of doing as the French have done, what amazing wealth, now stagnating and useless, will, by circulation, become productive!

After satisfying my curiosity in the cathedral, with the edifice, the treasures, and, above all with the paintings, I ascended the tower to take a view of the city and of the surrounding country. The prospect is extensive, and highly interesting. You look down upon a vale plentifully watered, wooded, and well cultivated, adorned with a rich variety of orchards and of corn-fields; yet, from the numerous habitations,

tations, appearing like one continued village. To the east, you see this valley open to the sea, but bounded in every other direction by distant mountains.

In the convents I found some good pictures, more especially in the following: in the two Carmelites, the Capuchins, the Dominicans, Franciscans, Augustines, the convent allotted to the nuns of Jerusalem, and the congregation of S. Philip Neri. In these, the artists whose works are most worthy to be admired are, Jacinto de Espinosa, Juan Bautista Juanes, Francisco Ribalta, Don Joseph Ramirez, Vicente Victoria, a disciple of Carlo Maratti, with many others, all natives of Valencia. In the church of San Juan de Mercado, the roof is painted in fresco by Palomino, who was likewise of Valencia. The famous Supper of Ribalta is in the college of Corpus Christi.

This seminary is worthy of attention, not merely for the pictures, which are beautiful, but for the library, which is well chosen, considering the age in which the patriarch of Antioch lived. He finished his college in the year 1604, and all the books were collected by himself. Among the relics in the sacristy, I took notice of a piece of sculpture, so minute, that in the size of an octavo volume it contained more than a hundred figures carved with the greatest elegance and truth.

In this college twenty-three masses are repeated daily for the dead, and for each the officiating priest receives four reals. In Spain few people of distinction die without making a provision for this purpose; but as the religious houses sometimes receive the legacy, and neglect the obligation connected with it, this proves a source of frequent litigation between the community and the friends of the deceased.

Of all the parish churches, not one, beside S. Nicholas, appeared worthy of attention. In this I admired the roof, executed in fresco, by Vidal, a disciple of Palomino, and the dome painted by Victoria. S. Thomas, of Villanueva, does credit to the pencil of Vergara. Three good pictures by Espinosa, and two by Juanes, of which one is the Last Supper, painted by that great master for the altar, must be reckoned among the finest pictures of Valencia.

The revenue of the religious houses is said to be considerable; but the most wealthy society in Valencia is the one last established; for when the convent of Montesa was destroyed by the earthquake of 1748, the monks removed their habitation, and settled here. They have lately fitted up their church with much taste, and at a considerable expence: this they can well afford, because, for the maintenance of four and twenty friars, they have a nett income of nine thousand pesos, or something less than fourteen hundred pounds a year.

The university of Valencia is a respectable community. It was founded at the solicitation of S. Vincent Ferrier, A. D. 1411; and soon after its institution, D. Alonso III. of Arragon, granted the privilege of nobility to all the students who should graduate in law. It was lately much on the decline; but the present rector has raised the reputation of his seminary, and they now reckon two thousand four hundred students. When I was at Valencia, he was just returned from Madrid with his new plan of study, approved of by his majesty.

jesty. (22d Dec. 1786.) The professors are seventy, viz. seven for the languages, including Latin, Greek, Hebrew, and Arabic; four for the mathematics, comprehending arithmetic, algebra, geometry, mechanics, hydrostatics, optics, astronomy, and experimental philosophy. In philosophy, including logic, metaphysics, moral philosophy, and physics, three permanent and as many temporary professors. In this branch they take father Jacquier for their guide. For medicine, with chemistry, they have eleven professors; six permanent, the other five changed at the end of three years. In this science they have adopted the best modern authors, such as, Beaumè, Macquer, Murray, Heister, Boerhaave, Home, Van-Swieten, and Cullen's Practice; but unfortunately, they have overlooked his best performance, which, without a question, is the Synopsis Nosologiæ Methodicæ; and they appear not to be acquainted with the works of Haller and of Gaubius. Like the medical school at Edinburgh, they have a clinical ward, visited daily by the students, and clinical lectures given by the professors. Beside these, with singular liberality of sentiment,

timent, they permit the profeffors to take what bodies they think proper from the hofpital, to be diffected by their furgeons.

For civil law, for canon law, and for ecclefiaftical difcipline, ten permanent profeffors are appointed, with nine affiftants, who are chofen for a time, and changed in rotation every year.

Eighteen profeffors, of which eleven are permanent, teach theology, including ecclefiaftical hiftory, and what they call theologia efcolaftico-dogmatica.

Thefe lectures begin the firft of October, end the laft of May, and are interrupted by as few holidays as the catholic religion will admit of.

During the month of June, all the ftudents are publicly examined in the lectures they have attended the preceding year; if approved, they receive their matriculation, and pafs on to a fuperior clafs; if not approved, they continue another year in the fame clafs, and being then found deficient, they are expelled the univerfity. To excite their emulation, prizes of books and money are propofed, and diftributed at the end of the examination, to thofe who have made the greateft progrefs in the fciences.

To graduate, if in arts, the student must, for a bachelor's degree, have obtained two matriculas, that is, he must have attended lectures two years, and must, at the public examination, have been twice approved; and to be master of arts, he must have gained three matriculas. In divinity and law, after four matriculas, he may claim his bachelor's degree; but to be doctor, he must have gained five. For the bachelor's degree in medicine, he must have attended the medical classes five years, and five times he must have passed his examinations. After this he must practise two years in the hospital before he can be admitted to his last degree. This certainly is an improvement on the plan pursued at Edinburgh, where three years study, or rather three years attendance on the lectures, and a slight examination, is all that is required for the degree of doctor. In Valencia, the candidate for this degree is privately examined by the professors. After this, if approved, he performs public exercises, and submits to a second examination. The professors then enter the chapel, and give their votes in private. If these are favourable, they proceed to examine

mine him once more in public, and if he acquits himself to their satisfaction, it is finally determined by vote that he shall be honoured with a degree.

The candidates for professorships form a distinct and separate class, and to be admitted into this, a man must have gained a certain number of matriculas in every science which can be useful in his line, and must pass a severe examination, both in public and in private. Thus, for instance, in medicine, to be what they call *opositor*, that is, to be admitted into the class of those who may be hereafter candidates for a vacant chair, whether permanent or temporary, he must have obtained two matriculas in Greek, two in mathematics, and one in the mechanics; he must defend a thesis, and be examined in every branch of medicine, by three censors at least, both in public and in private. After the examination, the censors with the rector enter the chapel, and having sworn before the altar to judge impartially, they decide by ballot whether the candidate be qualified or not. If all his exercises meet with their approbation, he is publicly received, invested

with

with the enfigns of his order, and immediately takes his feat among the profeffors of the univerfity.

From this clafs alone all vacant chairs are filled; and from the *opofitors* are taken the correctors of the univerfity prefs. Whilft thus employed they receive a falary. When a chair is vacant, it is filled by oppofition; that is, it is given to him, among the competitors, who, upon a ftrict examination, is judged to be moft worthy of it.

The falaries are moderate. The rector of the univerfity has thirty pounds a year; the vice-rector, fifteen. The permanent profeffors have in general forty pounds a year, but the profeffors of chemiftry receive fixty; the anatomift has fifty for falary, with ten for thirty diffections; and he who gives lectures on the practice of medicine is allowed feventy-five. The temporary profeffors, twenty-four in number, receive no more than fifteen pounds per annum.

This eftablifhment being in a ftate of infancy, it has been thought expedient to offer premiums to the profeffors who excel. After twelve years unremitted application

plication to the duties of his office, if any one shall write usefully on the science of which he is professor, he is to receive an additional pension of ten pounds; and if, after twenty years, he shall produce any valuable work, he will be entitled to an additional pension of twenty pounds: but should he compose an improved system, such as may be usefully adopted in his class, he will be entitled to a pension for life of thirty pounds a year, in addition to the former, on condition that he resigns his property in that work to the community.

The profits of the university press are designed, in the first place, to compose a fund of three thousand pounds. Of the surplus produce, sixty pounds a year is to be reserved for purchasing books, after which the residue will be equally divided every fourth year between the rectors, professors, librarians, and correctors of the press.

Their library contains many thousand volumes, mostly modern and well chosen, all collected by D. Francisco Perez Bayer, and presented by him to this university. At his table at Madrid I had frequently met the rector, and was therefore happy in renewing

newing our acquaintance at Valencia. He did me the honour to conduct me through the library, and shewed me a valuable collection of pictures in his own apartments. They are principally the works of the best masters of Italy and Florence; but among them he has some capital performances of Juanes.

The rector is a man of profound learning, and very zealous for the advancement of science in his community. For this purpose he undertook a journey to Madrid, and to him must be ascribed all the recent regulations, with the incomparable plan of study laid down in the royal edict to which I have referred. These do much credit to his understanding, and if carried into execution, will make this seminary one of the most respectable in Europe.

Beside the library of the university, four galleries in the archbishop's palace are devoted to the same purpose, and contain thirty-two thousand volumes, among which are many modern publications in every branch of literature. The rudiments of this collection, at the expulsion of the Jesuits, about the year 1759, consisted only of of their spoils; but the worthy prelates, who have been honoured with the crosier in this city, have swelled the catalogue by the addition of not a few among the many valuable productions which have appeared in Europe since the commencement of the present century.

Should literature revive in Spain, I am inclined to think it will be at Valencia. Men of genius are not wanting there; and whenever they shall take the pen, no press can do more justice to their works, than the one established in that city. Whoever has had an opportunity of seeing a valuable work of Francis Perez Bayer on the Hebræo-Samaritan coins, printed by *Montfort*, will agree with me in opinion, that no nation can boast of a superior work.

In traversing the city, to view whatever was most worthy of attention; considering its flourishing condition, and the opulence of the citizens, whether merchants, manufacturers, ecclesiastics, the military, or gentlemen of landed property, I was struck with the sight of poverty, of wretchedness, and of rags, in every street. The hospicio, or general workhouse, provides for two hundred

hundred and twenty men, one hundred and fifty boys, two hundred and eighty women, and ninety girls, who are all well fed, well clothed, well lodged; yet the city fwarms with fturdy beggars. I fufpected, however, what I found to be the cafe, that the ecclefiaftics diftribute money, and that the convents adminifter bread and broth every day at noon to all who make application at their gates. This circumftance will fufficiently account for the multitude of miferable objects, who in Valencia, as in all places, bear exact proportion to the undiftinguifhing benevolence of wealth. When in health, the moft lazy can never be in want of bread; and when ill, they have an hofpital always open to receive them. Should the indolent and vicious be inclined to abandon their offspring, the fame hofpital will provide for the helplefs infant a cradle and a grave.

I took an account of the patients and foundlings of the preceding year, ending the 31ft of December, 1786.

Of the peafants and common people, they received in the general hofpital four thoufand eight hundred. Of thefe, three

thoufand

thousand nine hundred and twenty-six went out, two hundred and thirty-five remained, and six hundred and thirty-nine died.

Of the military, eight hundred and ninety entered, seven hundred and eighty-two went out cured, eighty-one remained, and only twenty-seven died.

The foundlings were, three hundred and thirty-two, and of this number there died one hundred and fifty-nine.

Thus we see, that of the military, one out of thirty-three died in the hospital; but of the common people, nearly one in seven. The difference arises from this circumstance, that the lower classes are hurried away to the hospital, when near death, to save the expence of burial.

Of the foundlings, little less than half die within the year.

One establishment deserves the highest commendation; it is a *monte pio*, or bank, for the assistance of farmers, who are unable to purchase seed. For this loan they pay no interest, the funds being furnished from the *espolios y vacantes* of the church, that is from the effects of metropolitans deceased, and from vacant benefices.

Such

Such an inftitution for the promotion of agriculture, and for the encouragement of induftry, confidering the poverty of farmers, and their univerfal want of capital, is certainly politic and wife. From the fame funds in Galicia, fifhermen are provided with boats and nets.

No city in Spain pays more attention to the arts than the city of Valencia. The public academy for painting, ftatuary, and architecture, is well attended, and many of the pupils feem to be rifing up to eminence.

To have good defigners is of the laft importance to their manufactures of filk, of porcelain, and for painted tiles.

The filk manufacture is the moft important, becaufe the moft natural to the foil and to the climate. A. D. 1718, they reckoned no more than eight hundred looms, but by taking off oppreffive taxes, trade advanced, the manufacture flourifhed, and before the year 1740, the weavers amounted to two thoufand. (v. Reftablecimiento de las Fabricas por D. Bernardo de Ulloa.) In the year 1769, Don Antonio Ponz reckoned in the city no fewer than three thoufand one hundred and ninety-five

looms,

looms, including one hundred and seven stocking frames, and in the whole province, three thousand four hundred and thirty-seven; which required six hundred and twenty-two thousand two hundred and fifty pounds of silk. The trade is still increasing; and a gentleman engaged in it assured me, that they have now five thousand silk looms, and three hundred stocking frames. Their silk is thirty per cent. cheaper than it is in France, yet they are not able to meet their rivals fairly in the market.

At Alcora, in the neighbourhood of Valencia, a manufacture of porcelain has been successfully established by Count d'Aranda, and deserves encouragement. I was much pleased with their imitation of gilding. It is very natural; and the manager informed me, that after many years trial it was found to be durable.

I was most delighted with the manufacture of painted tiles. In Valencia, their best apartments are floored with these, and are remarkable for neatness, for coolness, and for elegance. They are stronger, and much more beautiful, than those we formerly received from Holland.

The

The commerce of Valencia is considerable. My much respected friend, the Abbé Cavanilles, states the produce of this fertile province, A. D. 1770, to have been sixty-five millions of livres, or £. 2,708,333. viz.

	Livres.
Dates	300,000
Figs, 60,000 quintals, a. 8	480,000
Flax, 30,000 ditto, a. 50	1,500,000
Hemp, 25,000 ditto, a. 40	1,000,000
Oil, 100,000 ditto, a. 45	4,500,000
Raisins, 60,000 ditto, a. 10	600,000
Rice, 140,000 load, a. 37	5,180,000
Silk, 2,000,000 pound, a. 15	30,000,000
Wool, 23,000 quintals, a. 40	920,000
Wine, 3,000,000 cantaros, a. 15 sols	2,250,000
Corn, such as wheat, oats, maize; oranges, lemons, almonds, pot-ash, carobs, esparto, salt, honey, fish, &c. &c.	18,270,000
	65,000,000

In this account I am inclined to think the brandy is omitted, as it is certainly too considerable to be included in one of the et ceteras. The quantity exported amounts
commonly

commonly to seven or eight thousand pipes, most of which comes to us through Guernsey as French brandy.

The silk, according to Bernardo Ward, is little more than one million pounds.

The usual exports from Valencia are,

Esparto rush, three or four cargoes for Italy and France.

Figs, two cargoes.

Hemp, only to Carthagena for the fleet.

Raisins, fifteen ships loaded with two thousand quintals each.

Wine, three or four thousand pipes.

Wool, about thirty thousand arrobas for Languedoc and Genoa.

Silk goods for America, one million two hundred thousand pounds weight.

But raw silk is not at present allowed to be exported, lest the price should be advanced, to the detriment of the manufacturer at home. The consequence of this absurd prohibition is, that,

1st, Great quantities are carried out by the illicit trader, whenever silk is wanted either in France or Portugal.

2d, The French have greatly increased their plantations of mulberries in Languedoc. The Italians and Portuguese have done the same in their dominions. Even the king of Prussia, in Silesia, has lately introduced this branch of husbandry, and cherished it with such attention, that in the year 1783 the produce was eleven thousand pound weights.

3d, The quantity produced in Spain is not only less, but the quality is worse, and the price to the manufacturer at home is higher than if the ports were open, and the trade were free. The maxim, on which the Spaniards have proceeded, was laid down by Colbert, when he put restraints upon the trade of corn, with a view to render provisions cheap, for the sake of manufactures. But experience has proved the folly of that expedient; for the English, by permitting the exportation of grain, increased the quantity, sunk the price, and brought the market nearer to a par. Previous to that period, wheat varied in its price between wide extremes, from sixteen guineas of our money to three shillings a quarter, or in old money, from a shilling to five pounds twelve. In proportion as liberty was granted to this commerce, the average price

of

of corn was found to sink, and the markets have been more regular.

The marquis de la Enfenada, A.D. 1752, permitted wheat, barley, rye, and maize, to pafs freely from one province to another; and in 1774, M. Turgot, whofe name will be had in everlafting rememberance, granted the fame liberty to France. The confequence was equally beneficial in both kingdoms. But notwithftanding their experience in the article of grain, all the nations of Europe, even the moft enlightened, have had contracted views, and by their impolitic reftrictions have done the greateft injury to agriculture, to manufactures, and to commerce. A fagacious writer on political œconomy has well obferved, that modern ftates appear feldom to think of more than one clafs of their fubjects at a time, and generally of the wrong clafs. For in prohibiting an export, *they think only of the buyers at home, whereas they ought then to think of the fellers there*; and in prohibiting an import, they think only of the feller at home and forget the buyers; the very reverfe of which ought to happen; becaufe, when the private fagacity of the fubject has taught him that he can make a gain in any fale, or a saving in any purchase, the state ought to facilitate his operations, which, in proportion to the extent of the concern, would produce a balance in favour of the country. It should always be remembered, that the demand creates the produce.

The immediate effects of permitting the free exportation of silk would be to raise the price; but then the increase of price would restrain the exportation, and by the encouragement thus given to the producer, tend to increase the quantity, and thereby ultimately to sink the price, till every thing had found its proper level. When the question is between the operations of agriculture and manufactures, Spain should never hesitate; but should by all means give the preference to the former, as most beneficial to the state.

No country, as far as positive injunctions can avail, has taken more pains to promote plantations of all kinds, but especially of mulberries, than Spain. By a royal edict, dated in the year 1567, commissioners were authorised, with their alguazil and escrivano, to make a progress through the country, and to compel, by penalties,

nalties, corporations to plant, in a time limited, their mountains and their waftrells, and private people to make hedge-rows, appointing both the kind of trees and the diftance at which they fhould be planted. But no provifion being made for nurferies, for fencing, and for watering the tender plants, the country ftill continues deftitute of trees. Indeed the national prejudice is fo ftrong againft them, as harbouring birds, and the vexations to which they fubject the owners of the foil are fo many, that few people are inclined to plant. Vifitors are appointed to watch the proprietors, and no one is permitted to cut down, even a decayed mulberry-tree, without a fpecial licence. Should he tranfgrefs, and take one for any domeftic purpofe, he muft bribe and feaft the vifitors, or he will be fubject to profecution and a fine.

In the royal edict for the regulation of plantations, publifhed A. D. 1748, are the fubfequent provifions:

§ 2. Intendants, in their regifters, fhall fpecify the number of trees of all kinds in their feveral diftricts.

§ 5. They fhall regifter the heads of families,

milies, and caufe each to plant annually three trees.

§ 15. The minifter of the marine fhall vifit perfonally the feveral diftricts, and examine the condition of thefe trees.

§ 20. No tree fhall be cut down for fewel, without a certificate from the efcrivano of the village that the tree is dead.

§ 23. Intendants fhall regulate the price of wood for fewel.

§ 30. No proprietor fhall prefume to cut any tree for building or repairs, without permiffion from the intendant. The written petition for this end muft fpecify the quantity required, and the purpofe for which it is folicited.

§ 31. The petition being directed to the fub-delegate of the intendant, fhall by him be forwarded to the *jufticia*, and having received from the court a certificate that the allegations are true, and pointing out the moft proper place for felling the number which is needful, fhall give permiffion for the fame, on condition that the proprietor fhall plant three for one.

Spanifh filk, from its inequality, is not in fuch requeft as that of other kingdoms;
yet

yet for some purposes it answers very well. For this reason our importation has commonly been trifling, and scarcely worthy of attention. In the year 1779, it amounted only to forty-four pounds and one-third, and the next year to sixty-five. But A. D. 1782 we took from them five hundred and forty-one pounds and one third, and the next year one thousand three hundred and thirty-nine pounds; after which, for three years, we received no more; but in the year 1784, we supplied them with six thousand three hundred and six pounds of raw silk; and four years after, we sent them five thousand seven hundred pounds of thrown silk, receiving from them in return three hundred and ninety-three pounds raw, and one hundred and forty-one thrown.

The quantity of wrought silks they took from us, on the average of six years, from 1783 to 1788 inclusive, as it appears by our custom-house books, was, in piece goods, one hundred and sixty-six pounds, in hose five hundred and seventy-eight pounds, mixed with inkle three hundred and seventy-nine pounds, and with worsted one thousand five hundred and six pounds. Their predilection is certainly in favour of the French, who, in point of taste, may with justice claim the preference. Formed on this model, by the assistance of their newly instituted school for painting, and with due encouragement from the Economical Society, the Valencian weavers must improve, and may be in time competitors with those of Lyons, who at present appear without a rival in the market.

If we may believe Bernardo Ward, time was, when Spain produced and employed in her own looms ten million pounds of silk; whereas at present she produces little more than one million, half of which is exported raw.

The *mulberry* of Valencia is the *white*, as being most suitable to a well-watered plain. In Granada they give the preference to the *black*, as thriving well in elevated stations, as more durable, more abundant in leaves, and yielding a much finer and more valuable silk. But then it does not begin bearing till it is about twenty years of age. In this province they reckon, that five trees should produce two pounds of silk.

I had the curiosity to examine their method

thod of feeding the silk-worms in Spain. These industrious spinners are spread upon wicker shelves, which are placed one above the other, all round, and likewise in the middle of, each apartment, so as to leave room only for the good woman to pass with their provisions. In one house I saw the produce of six ounces of seed, and was informed, that to every ounce during their feeding season, they allow sixty arrobas of leaves, valued at two pounds five. Each ounce of seed is supposed to yield ten pounds of silk, at twelve ounces to the pound. March 28, the worms began to hatch; and, May 22, they went up to spin. In the intermediate space, on the eleventh day, they slept; and on the fourteenth, they awoke to eat again, receiving food twice a day till the twenty-second day. Having then slept a second time, without interruption, for three days, they were fed thrice a day, and thus alternately continued eating eight days and sleeping three, till the forty-seventh day; after which they eat voraciously for ten days, and not being stinted, consumed sometimes from thirty to fifty arrobas in four and twenty hours. They then climbed

up

up into rosemary bushes, fixed for that purpose between the shelves, and began to spin.

Upon examination, they appear evidently to draw out two threads by the same operation, and to glue these together, covering them with wax. This may be proved by spirit of wine, which will dissolve the wax, and leave the thread. Having exhausted her magazine, the worm changes her form, and becomes a nymph, till on the seventy-first day, from the time that the little animal was hatched, when she comes forth with plumage, and having found her mate, begins to lay her eggs. At the end of six days from this period of existence, having answered the end of their creation, they both lie down and die. This would be the natural progress; but, to preserve the silk, the animal is killed by heat, and the cones being thrown into boiling water, they begin winding off the silk.

Silk-worms, in close rooms, are much subject to disease; but in the open air, as in China, they are not only more healthy and more hardy, but make better silk. It appears to be precisely the same with them, as with the sick confined in hospitals, or foundlings shut up in work-houses. For this reason the ingenious Abbé Bertholon recommends procuring from China some of the wild silk-worms, and leaving them in the open air, protected only by a shed from rain. He is persuaded that the race might thus be made so hardy, in process of time, as to survive all the variations of the seasons.

In China, they have three kinds of silk-worm, two living on the leaves of the ash and of the oak; the third, thriving best on a species of the pepper-tree, called fagara, whose silk, remarkable for strength, washes like linen, and is not apt to be greased.

The progress of this article of luxury in Europe, after it had been introduced from Asia by two monks, who brought worms to Constantinople, was very slow. There, and in Greece, it continued little noticed by the rest of Europe, from the year 551 of the christian æra, till Roger II. king of Sicily, pillaged Athens, A. D. 1130, and brought silk-worms to Palermo. From thence they were speedily conveyed to Italy and Spain; but, till the reign of Queen Elizabeth, silk-stockings were unknown in England;

England; and with refpect to Scotland, there is in being a M S. letter from James VI. to the Earl of Mar, requefting the loan of a pair, in which the Earl had appeared at court, becaufe he was going to give audience to the French ambaſſador.

Silk is certainly the moſt confiderable article produced in the province of Valencia, being nearly equal to all the reſt together, and, if properly encouraged, would yield inexhauſtible treafures to this kingdom. No one, who has feen the Spaniards on the fea-coaſt, can think them lazy; and as for foil, for climate, and for local advantages, few countries, if any, can be compared to this.

[The land in this fertile valley never reſts; for no fooner is one crop removed, than the farmer begins to prepare it for another.] They plough with one horfe, and never attempt any thing more than to pulverife the foil; for which purpofe their implement is admirably calculated, confidering that they move the earth eight or ten times a year. In this kind of hufbandry they have neither occafion to turn the fod, nor time to let it rot, and therefore could de-

rive

rive no advantage from the coulter, the fin, and the mouldboard of our ploughs. Whilſt I was paſſing through the valley, and in my excurſions round the city, I obſerved them earthing up their maize with hoes larger than our common ſpades. This inſtrument is well adapted to their ſoil, their culture, and their crops. In this operation they work hard, and make diſpatch.

The beds, into which they divide the land, are very large, and perfectly flat. The water covers the whole ſurface, ſtagnates for a few days, and is then diſcharged.

To ſhew the exceeding fertility of this vale, I ſhall ſubjoin a conciſe deſcription of the crops, with reſpect to the time of ſowing and of reaping, which will point out their ſucceſſion, and I ſhall give the medium produce of wheat, barley, oats, Indian corn, and rice, in proportion to the ſeed.

Wheat is put into the ground the beginning of November, and is reaped the middle of June, when they obtain from twenty to forty for one.

Barley is ſown in October, and in May they
receive

receive from eighteen to twenty four for one.

Oats are in the ground from the middle of October to the middle of June, and yield from twenty to thirty for one.

Maize follows the barley, as the second crop in the same year, and with a favourable season gives, at the end of October, a hundred for one.

Rice, commonly sown about the first of April, is transplanted in June, and in October rewards the farmer forty fold in proportion to his seed.

Garbanzos (the cicer of Linnæus) are drilled about the month of January, and come off the ground the latter end of June.

Guisantes (pisum sativum) occupy the land from September to April and May.

Beans may be put into the ground, either early in the autumn, or in the beginning of the year.

Hemp seed is scattered on the land in April, and is cleared about the middle of July.

The intermediate crops are, cabbages, cauliflowers, carrots, parsneps, French beans, leeks, garlick, onions, turnips, artichokes, tomatos,

tomatos, lettuces, capsicums, cucumbers, melons, four species of the *calabaza* (cucurbita laginaria) and sandias (a species likewise of cucurbita) with a variety of esculents, whose names do not occur to me.

Thus, with a warm sun, plenty of water, and a rich choice of crops, suited to every season of the year, the grateful earth repays the labour of the husbandman at least three times in the course of twelve or thirteen months.

The rock, wherever it appears in this vicinity, is calcarious. At Picacente, two leagues from the city, clean chalk abounds. Limestone and good marble are procured from all the mountains; and it is worthy to be noticed, that Mr. Bowles discovered quicksilver in calcarious rock, both here and near to San Felipe. How far the connection holds between these substances in other countries I am not competent to say; but in Spain, as I conceive, no instance has been known of cinnabar, either in granite or in schist.

The recommendation with which Count Florida Blanca was pleased to honour me, was to the Duke of Crillon, governor and captain general of the province. Under his protection I could not be otherwife than happy. I had accefs to him at all hours, dined with him almoft every day; and when he was at leifure, I enjoyed the pleafure of his converfation; but when bufinefs called for his attention, he turned me over to the ladies. Here I met with the principal people of Valencia, who were either invited to his table in the middle of the day, or frequented the tertulia in the evening.

Among the remarkable characters I met with at the palace, the moft fingular was a little boy under training at a convent for the pulpit, who was fent for, that I might have an opportunity of feeing him. He was not more than twelve years of age; yet his judgment, memory, and imagination were fo mature, that without any fpecial preparation, he was able to expatiate with propriety on whatever fubject was propofed to him; and fuch were his natural powers as an orator, that his periods were harmonious, his expreffion nervous, his delivery graceful, and his arguments

ments well chosen. Although the room was filled with genteel company, he was not abashed; nor did his attention appear to be distracted by the variety of objects and amusements in which they were engaged. Upon enquiry, I found that the fathers of his convent, perceiving him to be a boy of singular abilities, had taken infinite pains with his education.

The favourite amusement of the duke is whist; but as he had never more than one table, the visitors in general joined in conversation. This was much more agreeable than the custom of some Spanish families, to make all their company sit down at one long table to spend the whole evening at some game that gives no employment, either to the memory, the judgment, or to any one of the mental faculties. The game they usually adopt is lottery.

Whenever any remarkable person came to the tertulia, the duke had the goodness to present me to him. As an ecclesiastic, I wished to be introduced to the archbishop, but he was not in town: he lived retired in the country. My curiosity was excited strongly by the various and discordant

dant characters given me of this prelate by those to whom I had applied for information. Some described him as a good fort of man, but rather too severe; others represented him as a monk, secluded from the world, austere in the extreme, and perfectly a misanthrope.

No sooner had I mentioned to the duke my desire of being introduced by a letter to this prelate, than he obligingly engaged to do more than I requested; for he sent over, made an appointment to spend a day with him at his country seat, and conveyed me thither in his carriage.

In the way we passed through Burjasot, where the Romans had their subterranean granaries. Thirty-seven of these still remain, and are filled with corn for the use of the city.

When we arrived at the archbishop's homely habitation, he received us with politeness, and I was delighted to find in the good old man all that ease and affability, that mildness and gentleness of manner, which became his dignity and age. Far from being morose, he was cheerful and engaging in his conversation, uncommonly

sensible

sensible and well informed. Being fond of study, he avoided the interruptions inevitable in such a city as Valencia; and, as a man of uncommon piety, he courted solitude; yet he was attentive to all the duties of his office, and occasionally entertained his friends. In a word, he appeared to me precisely what a bishop ought to be.

As we returned, conversing with the duke on the satisfaction I had received from this short acquaintance with the archbishop, he confirmed my ideas of his character, and well accounted for his having been represented by some as uncommonly severe. This prelate, considering Valencia as a commercial city, had opposed the construction of a theatre, because he thought both the dissipation and the expence attendant on the diversions of the stage, unfriendly to the prosperity of trade. The duke himself seemed inclined to favour this opinion; at least he agreed to compromise the matter, and instead of being established in the city, he suffered the players to pitch their tents on the sea-side, at the village of the *Gras*, within a moderate distance from Valencia.

Thither

Thither the duke had the goodnefs to carry me, with his dutchefs and his amiable daughter. The theatre is a fpacious edifice, conftructed like a barn, but covered only with efparto mats, which, as they have no need to be afraid of rain, is fully fufficient for the purpofe. The company was genteel, and the actors were by no means contemptible. They reprefented that afternoon the Deluge, in which the devil was the principal character. The piece itfelf was highly ludicrous; and when the curtain dropped, the devil, with a daughter-in-law of Noah, at the requeft of the dutchefs, concluded the whole by dancing a fandango.

Under fuch powerful protection as that of the duke of Crillon, who, in authority and ftile of living, is little lefs than viceroy, I faw every thing to the greateft poffible advantage. This was peculiarly ferviceable, when the knights of the Royal Maeftranza celebrated a feftival in honour of the infant don Antonio. Of thefe knights, four companies, confifting of the principal nobility, are eftablifhed in the four cities of Granada, Seville, Ronda, and Valencia, each diftinguifhed by a peculiar uniform. Like the

the feudal barons, they are bound, with their vaſſals, to attend the king in perſon when he goes to war. Their military exerciſe is derived from remote antiquity. On this feſtival they aſſembled in a ſpacious area, incloſed for the occaſion; at the upper end of which was the picture of the ſovereign, behind a curtain. The knights, mounted on beautiful and high bred Andaluſian horſes, marched in order to the picture, the curtain was withdrawn, and inſtantly every ſword was brandiſhed in the air. Having thus paid their homage to the ſovereign, they performed, with ſurpriſing regularity, their various evolutions, in the ſame manner and form as was done at Aranjuez. This being accompliſhed, they prepared themſelves for other feats of activity and ſkill. For this purpoſe, an image of Minerva, placed near the gallery in which the ladies were aſſembled, held one riband, whilſt another, oppoſite to this, with a bunch of flowers, was fuſpended from the beak of an eagle. Things being thus arranged, each of the knights, clapping ſpurs to his horſe, and forcing him to full ſpeed, directed the point of his well

poiſed

poised lance with such address, that few of them failed to pierce both ribands at their first attempts. After this atchievement, twice performed by every knight, they again repeated their evolutions, saluted the picture of the king once more, the curtain was drawn, and all retired in the same order in which they had arrived, with trumpets, kettle-drums, and martial music.

This being the festival of St. *Anthony* of Padua, in honour of the day, and as a compliment to the infant don *Antonio*, who is *hermano mayor*, that is, grand master, or president of this military order, his lieutenant, don *Antonio Salabert*, gave a *refresco* in the evening.

The company consisted of six hundred, selected from the highest classes in Valencia. The gentlemen were assembled in one room, in the other the ladies sat arranged in order, like tulips in a garden. As I had the honour to attend the captain general, I partook of his peculiar privilege, and, with him, paid a visit to the ladies. It was a pleasing sight. They were all in *gala*, many of them elegantly dressed, and adorned in a splendid manner with pearls, with gold, and

and with the moſt coſtly gems. When they had been for ſome time aſſembled, ſervants entered, firſt with a variety of ices; then, after conſiderable intervals, with cakes and chocolate; and finally, with cold water. The ladies were all firſt ſerved, then the gentlemen partook of a ſimilar refreſco. By the time that theſe had finiſhed their refreſhment, it was more than midnight, although we had aſſembled early in the evening. The ſervants then retired, a band of muſic, vocal and inſtrumental, entered, and performed a little opera, written for the occaſion, called Peace between Mars and Cupid.

Such refreſcos are given by people of high faſhion on their nuptial day; and ſuch a one was given by the brother of count Florida Blanca, whilſt I was at Madrid; but as I had not the honour to be preſent on that occaſion, I felt the higher ſatisfaction in the ſight of this.

After I had been ſome days at Valencia, at the earneſt requeſt of the duke, I viſited a friend, for whom he had a particular eſteem, in order to determine a diſpute between the attending phyſician and a young chirurgeon, who occaſionally ſaw him. As the latter was under the immediate protection of the duke, it was partly with a view to save his credit, that I was desired to give my judgment on the case. The duke, therefore, conveyed me in his carriage to the habitation of his friend, and the young chirurgeon joined the party. The patient complained of a cough, accompanied with spitting; and the question to be determined was, whether the disease were phthisis, or merely a catarrh?

My enquiries were confined to the usual symptoms of a hectic; and not finding, from the account the patient gave me of himself, any one of these, I did not hesitate to pronounce him free from phthisis, to the satisfaction of the duke, and the no small triumph of the chirurgeon.

But when I returned, towards the close of day, I had reason, from the increase of fever, and from the characteristic flushing of his cheeks, to think that he had, to obtain a favourable opinion, concealed many of his symptoms. I requested, therefore, that I might have a conference with his physician, and was happy to find that he had expressed the same desire. When
we

we had the satisfaction of meeting the next day, in the presence of his patient, he directed his discourse to me in Latin, and with the greatest fluency gave me the history of this disease, which began with pleurisy, and was in its progress attended with a remittent fever, night sweats, and the other characteristic symptoms of a hectic. It was then too clear that the patient had deceived himself, and that the meek and too easily brow-beaten physician was well founded in his diagnosis. He thanked me with expressions of humility for giving him the meeting; but he evidently wanted spirit to enjoy his triumph. I found him modest, yet sensible, and, for a Spanish physician, well informed; that is, acquainted with the works of Boerhaave, but not with modern publications.

I have observed in general, that the physicians, with whom I have had occasion to converse, are disciples of their favourite doctor Piquer, who denied, or at least doubted of, the circulation of the blood. Yet they begin to get acquainted with the names of Van Swieten, Hoffmann, Sauvage, Gaubius, de Haen, and Cullen. They have

have indeed laboured under the greateſt diſadvantages in their education, and in the want of encouragement when they entered upon practice, receiving little money, and leſs honour, in the way of their profeſſion. In their medical claſſes they had no diſſections, no experiments in chemiſtry, and for botany they were unacquainted with Linnæus. Theſe defects will now be remedied. But even in the preſent day, the fee of the phyſician is, two pence from the tradeſman, ten pence from the man of faſhion, and nothing from the poor. Some of the noble families agree with a phyſician by the year, paying him annually fourſcore reals, that is, ſixteen ſhillings, for his attendance on them and on their families.

They all acknowledge that the monks are more liberal than people of the firſt faſhion, more eſpecially if confidence and ſecreſy are needful.

In point of honour, no claſs of citizens meets with leſs reſpect than the phyſicians; but in proportion as the nation ſhall acquire wealth, they will riſe up in conſequence, and be regarded with eſteem.

Of one thing, which in Spain is required

quired from chirurgeons and phyſicians, I have never been able to find any one who could give me a ſatisfactory account. Before they enter into their profeſſion, they are obliged to ſwear, that they will defend the immaculate conception of the Bleſſed Virgin. This requiſition is the more extraordinary, becauſe that point is not univerſally agreed upon, even between catholics themſelves; yet many centuries may paſs before the medical tribe will be freed from this unreaſonable impoſition. To give due weight to the ſanction of an oath, every country ſhould purge away thoſe which are become obſolete, but more eſpecially ſuch as are univerſally regarded as abſurd.

Converſing with ſeveral phyſicians in this part of Spain, who have made uſe of the cicuta with manifeſt advantage in caſes of glandular obſtructions, I was led to a conjecture, that the virtues of this plant depend much on the ſoil and climate in which it is produced. In England, as I imagine, the beneficial effects have not anſwered the expectations raiſed by the report of the adventurous phyſician, by whom it was firſt recommended to the notice of the world.

world. Something similar is found in Spain; for in the province of Valencia, the cicuta has been given successfully for tumors supposed to be cancerous; whereas about Madrid they have derived no advantage from its use; and it has been observed, that in Castille, the cicuta is aromatic, sweet, and free from every nauseous quality; but in Valencia, and all along the eastern coast of Spain, it is fetid and loathsome, affects the head, and, in large doses, proves a powerful emetic. We may readily conceive that, where the sensible qualities are so various and discordant, the medical effects cannot perfectly agree. The physicians on this coast increase their dose from a few grains of the extract up to half an ounce.

The air and climate of Valencia would be highly beneficial to the English in a variety of cases, more especially for nervous, hysterical, and hypocondriac disorders, for shattered constitutions, and for those who suffer either by a redundancy, or a suppression of the bile. These would find the oranges and grapes most powerful detergents; and every article of food, whether

animal

animal or vegetable, being light and easy of digestion, the most delicate stomach would never feel oppressed. In our island these patients suffer by humidity; but in Valencia, such is the dryness of the air, that sugar and salt may be constantly exposed without contracting the least sign of moisture.

As a winter's residence, and throughout the spring, no city can be more delightful than Valencia; and I believe few cities can boast of more agreeable society. Had I sought amusement, I might have had introductions to as many pleasant families as a stranger could wish to cultivate; but as information was the first object of my pursuit, I confined myself chiefly to the duke of Crillon's, where every distinguished character resorted, and to M. Thomas Vague's, from whom, as well as from his amiable nephew, don Joseph Boneli, I was certain of receiving the most accurate accounts of every thing relating to the agriculture, manufactures, and commerce of the country. Had the count de Lumiaris been at leisure to bestow upon me more of his conversation, my happiness at Valencia would have been complete.

The

The government of Valencia is not distinguished from that of other provinces. The captain general presides in the civil, criminal, and military courts, and the intendant has the sole authority in matters of finance. The city is governed by its own corregidor, assisted by two alcaldes mayores and twenty-four regidors, with four deputies from the commons, and two syndics.

The court of the inquisition has three judges, with a nuncio extraordinary, and twenty-two *secretarios del secreto*, who are paid out of the confiscated effects of persons condemned by their tribunal.

The taxes are heavy in Valencia. Every thing entering the city, even cloths made at Madrid, and silk for the manufactures, and all commodities without distinction, pay eight per cent. upon their value. But the province at large is free from some oppressive contributions to which other provinces continue subject, paying six hundred twelve thousand and twenty-eight pesos, or ninety-one thousand eight hundred and four pounds, as an equivalent for the provincial rents, purveyance, and forage for the army, with the royal monopolies of brandy and of salt.

salt. To this commutation may be in part attributed the prosperous condition of the whole kingdom of Valencia.

This city was formerly oppressed by the nobility; but after the rebellion of 1520, when all the nobles were expelled, and thirteen regidors were chosen from the commons to render impartial justice; although in this conflict the commons were ultimately subdued, and had the mortification to see all their leaders either slain in the field of battle, or by the hands of the executioner suffering cruel torments and an ignominious death; yet from that period their tyrants were impressed with terror, and became cautious how they should rekindle a flame, by which they themselves had nearly been consumed.

They have at present little more to ask than freedom to their commerce. With this, and with a certainty that the peace and protection they enjoy, shall not be subject to the caprices of a weak sovereign, or of a wicked minister, Valencia would soon be ranked among the most commercial cities of the continent.

The weights and measures of this province differ much from those received in other parts of Spain. The vara is longer than that of Castille; twelve of the former being equal to thirteen of the latter. Their celemines bear the same proportion.

In agriculture, nine palms make a *braza*, and twenty brazas, equal to forty-one varas, make the cord with which they measure land. Two hundred square brazas make a fanega, and six fanegas, equal to about half an acre, make a cahizada. Six cahizadas make a yugada.

In corn measure, the cahiz contains twelve *barchillas*, or forty-eight *celemines*.

The *carga* of wine contains fifteen *arrobas*, or cantaras, and is equal to sixty *azumbres*; but the *carga* of oil is only twelve *arrobas*.

The pound consists of twelve, sixteen, eighteen, or thirty-six ounces, according to the article in question, whether bread, fresh fish, salt fish, or butcher's meat. In like manner, the arroba may be of thirty, of thirty-two, or thirty-six pounds, each pound being twelve ounces.

When

When I was about to leave Valencia, I enquired the price of provisions, which I found to be as undermentioned, the pound being of thirty-six ounces.

Beef, twenty quartos; veal, twenty-six.

Mutton and pork, thirty-six.

Bread, four quartos for sixteen ounces.

JOURNEY

FROM

VALENCIA to BARCELONA.

WHEN I was making arrangements for my departure from Valencia, an amiable young friend, Don Joseph Boneli, was so polite and attentive as to offer me his company, and a place in his carriage, as far as Morviedro. This offer I gladly accepted; yet I quitted, with much regret, a city in which I had enjoyed the most agreeable society.

June 21, we set forward on our journey. In the way we examined a stately edifice, called the convent *de los Reyes*, erected and endowed by the last Duke of Calabria for his monument, and as a provision for sixty monks, who are bound to say mass daily for the repose of his soul. For this service they

they have an ample recompenfe, enjoying a revenue, by their own confeffion, of twenty thoufand pefos, equal to three thoufand pounds, a year, but fuppofed to be confiderably more.

Their convent is truly magnificent; the marble pillars are moft beautiful; their pictures are many of them excellent, painted chiefly by Juanes, Ribalta, and Zariñena. The treafures of their church are far removed from mediocrity; but that which is moft worthy of attention is a collection of manufcripts, tranfmitted to the founder from his remote progenitors, confifting of two hundred and fifty volumes in good prefervation, and highly illuminated, like the beft of the old Roman miffals. They are chiefly the works of the fathers, with many of the claffics, among which is an elegant copy of Livy, in five volumes folio; the two firft in Latin, the others in Italian.

At the diftance of about three leagues from the city is Puzol, where the archbifhop has a celebrated garden. We turned afide to view it, but were much difappointed in our expectations. In the infancy of fcience, this humble attempt deferved commendation;

mendation; but in the present day it has little to attract attention.

All the way from Valencia to Morviedro, the lower lands are watered, and produce much silk, wheat, barley, maize, and alfalfa, with a variety of leguminous plants. The higher lands are shaded by the algarrobo, the olive, and the vine. The whole country is well inhabited, and scarcely can you travel half a league without passing through a village.

Morviedro is a considerable city, containing five thousand one hundred and twenty-six inhabitants, who are strangers to manufactures, and depend altogether for subsistence on the produce of the soil. The commerce of this city is chiefly in oil, raisins, wine, and brandy. The wine is delicate, and far from dear. Mr. Thomas Vague delivers it aboard at fifty-four pesos the ton, which is forty shillings and six pence the hogshead. To make one hogshead of brandy, they commonly distil four hogsheads of ordinary wine, and when distilled to what is denominated Holland's proof, it is sold for exportation at two pounds seventeen shillings the hogshead.

The

The antiquities of Morviedro, formerly Saguntum, have been often and well described by others. They are in a ſtile of ſuch magnificence, that even they who have no taſte for antiquities, as ſuch, muſt be pleaſed with theſe.

The theatre, vaſt in its dimenſions, and capable of receiving near ten thouſand people, is hewn out of the rock, and commands a moſt extenſive proſpect of the ſubjacent country, which is bounded by the ſea.

Aſcending to the ſummit of the mountain, and looking to the ſouth, the eye is raviſhed with the ſight of Valencia, ſtanding like a queen ſurrounded by her ſubjects. The villages appear to be innumerable, and all the intermediate country is one continued garden.

June 22, in the morning, I took leave of my valuable friend Boneli, and proceeded on my journey in a calecine, attended only by the guide, to whom the little vehicle belonged, paſſing along the Huerta, with the ſea on the right, and high lime-ſtone mountains on the left. From this Huerta, having croſſed a mountain near the ſea, we entered another, which is extenſive, well watered,

watered, and, like the former, bounded by diftant mountains to the left. On the declivity of one of them ftands Villa Vieja, with its elevated caftle, famous for hot fprings. The rocks are gypfum and limeftone.

The vallies produce grain, figs, grapes, olives, and filk, in great abundance.

In the morning I paffed through *Nules*, a city containing three thoufand three hundred and thirty-eight fouls. It is a marquifate now in abeyance, the title being difputed by feventeen claimants. Within the walls are two convents, two hermitages, and a parifh church. One of the convents, although finifhed thirty years, is not yet inhabited, confequently the revenue is difpofed of by the archbifhop, and applied to pious ufes.

The city is governed by two alcaldes, the one ftiled mayor, the other menor, affifted by four regidors, who continue only for a year, and then choofe their fucceffors, fubject to the approbation of the marquis; or rather, they name fix for the office of alcalde, and eight for regidors, out of which the marquis makes choice of the proper number.

number. In the royal boroughs, the magistrates, in like manner, nominate fit persons to succeed them, but then the royal audiencia, or supreme court of justice and civil government in Valencia, from this return select the persons best qualified, or most approved by government, to fill the vacant offices. To this city belong three dependant villages, whose inhabitants are *vicinos*, or citizens of Nules.

I observed here a number of caves, said to be five hundred, from eight to twelve feet diameter, and from twelve to twenty deep. They are sunk in the limestone rock, and were designed for granaries. That purpose they at present serve, and the collector of the tithes makes use of thirty for depositing his wheat. He informed me, that he rented the tithes of corn, wine, and oil; but he lamented, that he had no claim on either silk or garlic, these being free from tithe, which he the more severely felt, because the produce of garlic is nearly equal to half the value of the corn. He told me, that he was administrator for the bank of S. Charles in supplying the troops with wheat and barley; and from him I find, that the bank has a profitable bargain.

The duke of Infantada has confiderable poffeffions in this vicinity, all of them in adminiftration, that is, cultivated on his account, but chiefly for the advantage of his ftewards, who are the greateft gainers.

Soon after dinner we paffed through *Villa Real*, a city of five thoufand fix hundred and fifty-eight inhabitants. Proceeding on our way towards Caftellon de la Plana, we croffed the Mijares, which fupplies water to the juftly celebrated aqueduct of Almafora.

Thus far the whole extent of road from Valencia is thirty feet wide, well formed, and in excellent condition. The foil is chiefly clay; the crops on the lower lands, wheat, barley, maize, leguminous plants, and melons, with mulberry trees in great abundance; the more elevated lands have olives; and the higheft are abandoned to the algarrobo. Their plough is ill-fuited to the foil, being the light one laft defcribed, drawn by one horfe in fhafts.

Caftellon de la Plana reckons ten thoufand
feven

seven hundred and thirty-three inhabitants, with one parish church, and six convents. The chapel of la Sangre is light, elegant, and well proportioned, fitted up entirely by a young artist, who is indebted to himself alone for the refinement of his taste, because he had no instructor, nor one good model in the place, by which he might improve.

Few villages can boast a richer collection of pictures. The major part are by Francisco Ribálta, who was a native of Castellon, and among those, the most admired are, his Purgatory, at the altar of *las Animas*; his S. Eloy and S. Lucia, in the church of the Augustins; S. Roque, in the *Hermita* or chapel dedicated to him, in which that saint is represented sitting under a tree, looking up to heaven, and receiving a cake of bread, brought to him by a dog. Beside these, we find several others equally worthy of admiration in the church of the Dominicans.

In the chapel of la Sangre are preserved some good pictures of Bergara; and the Capuchins are much indebted to Zurbaran for some of his best works.

At

At the altar of the great church is the Assumption of the Blessed Virgin, by Carlo Maratti.

When I arrived at *Castellon*, I made inquiries about the aqueduct of Almafora, by which all this extensive plain receives water from the Mijares. They informed me, that I had crossed it soon after I passed the new bridge over that river, but as it is a tunnel almost the whole distance from S. Quiteria to Almafora, we crossed it without being sensible that we had done so. Considering that this tunnel is through a rock of limestone, and that it was executed in the year 1240, it deserves to be regarded as stupendous. In comparison with this, how contemptible is the Montagne Percée, in Languedoc, for which Lewis XIV. received the most fulsome adulation!

This useful aqueduct of Almafora has been attributed both to the Romans and to the Moors; but I am well informed that Jayme el Conquistador is alone entitled to the praise.

June 23. At five in the morning we left Castellon de la Plana, and descending to a

plain,

plain, we approached the mountains and the sea, till we came to *las Casas de Venicase*. Here I stopped a few minutes to admire an elegant church lately built by my learned friend Don F. P. Bayer, designed, as I imagine, for the protection of his monument.

From Venicase we ascended between the mountains, on which I observed rosemary, thyme, lavender, the palmito, juniper, and algarrobo, with the beautiful nerium oleander in abundance. The American aloe in the vallies, every where in blossom, with its lofty pyramid of florets rising to the height of more than twenty feet, attracted particular attention.

At a little distance on the right we discovered Oropesa, with its castle, occupying the summit of a pointed rock. In this an alcaid is stationed with a garrison, and two pieces of cannon, to protect the country from the incursions of the Algerines.

Under this fortress extends a plain, covered every where with vines or grain. A few almonds, figs, and algarrobos, serve to shew what the country might produce; but unfortunately, the industry of the farmer is not properly encouraged, and the whole plain continues deftitute of water, although by norias it might be abundantly fupplied.

At eleven in the forenoon we took refreshment in a *venta* belonging to the monks of S. Antonio of Valencia. Here the norias evidently prove that water may be eafily procured, and that when procured it never fails producing the moft luxuriant crops.

All the villages in this vicinity belong to the bifhop of Tortofa, who claims and exercifes a temporal dominion, appointing the magiftrates, and receiving three thirty-fevenths of their wheat, barley, and oil, with three-fortieths of their wine. Befide thefe dues, the farmer pays one-thirty-feventh of his grain, and one in forty of his wine, to the curate of the parifh. Some articles are free, as for inftance, in one village nothing is paid for maize; in the diftrict of another, the fame immunity is claimed for pigs and algarrobos.

Here the travelling fheep of Arragon find pafture in the winter, and pay to the parifh of Cavanes eighteen hundred pefos,

or

or two hundred and seventy pounds a year, beside making satisfaction for the injury they may do the wheat.

Many villages have been totally ruined by the depredations of the Moors, and the inhabitants have sought refuge in Cavanes, or in other places more easy of defence.

Torreblanca is going to decay, but *Alcala de Chivet*, or *Gisvert*, having received inhabitants from many deserted villages, now contains seven hundred families. The distance of this town from Torreblanca is called one league; but as we were more than two hours on the road, I reckon the league to be at least seven miles.

Alcala belongs to the military order of Montesa, and was given to the late infant Don Louis; but at his death it reverted to the crown. The beneficiary or military tenant receives the tithes, and nominates the magistrates. The tithes, as they are called, are not the same to all the inhabitants, because the farmers from many abandoned villages, having sought refuge and protection here, they continue to pay the same proportion as was exacted from them, previous to their removal. Hence,

whilst

whilst some are acquitted for a tenth, others are obliged to pay an eighth, a seventh, or even three-nineteenths.

I was much pleased with the parish church. The front is elegant, adorned with columns and numerous images, and the inside, consisting of three iles, and one great dome with eight lesser ones, is beautifully fitted up, and furnished with good pictures. Ample provision is made for the support of fourteen priests, who daily officiate at eleven altars.

The common lands are depastured by the sheep of Arragon, yet the market is not supplied with mutton, and as for beef it is rarely seen in Alcala. Bread is sold at four quartos for eleven ounces.

June 24, at four in the morning, we renewed our journey, and descending between two elevated chains of limestone mountains, came to *Benicarlo*, on the sea-coast, at the distance of four leagues from Alcala. The soil is peculiarly favourable for the cultivation of the vine, and produces a generous wine, much used for enriching the poorer wines in the neighbourhood of Bourdeaux, for the purpose of making claret.

Mr.

Mr. Macdonell sells this wine at thirty-five pesos, or five guineas, the pipe; and a most elegant white wine, made by simple pressure, for thirty-four pesos the hogshead, or ten pounds four shillings the pipe. This delicate wine is all disposed of before Christmas. Brandy is sold for the same price as the red wine.

This city, containing three thousand and sixty-three inhabitants, belongs to the knights of Montesa, who nominate the magistrates and claim the tithes. Wine pays four thirty-fourths, but all other articles a tenth, excepting maize and algarrobos, which are free. Of the tithe of wine a canon of Tortosa takes one half, the military tenant and the curate each enjoy a quarter. In all this country the greatest variety is found in the proportion of the tithe, and in the exemptions enjoyed by different parishes. No two perfectly agree in one common rule.

From Benicarlo we traversed an extensive plain, with high mountains on our left, and on our right the sea. As we approached the confines, cultivation ceased; but no sooner had we entered Catalonia, than we

again

again admired a well watered country, and luxuriant crops. The rich vallies produce wheat, barley, maize, hemp, flax, figs, walnuts, filk; the higher lands, olives and wine. It is Sunday; yet the farmers are at work.

In the way we took notice of three monumental croffes, of which the moft recent marked the fpot where a traveller had been robbed and murdered the preceding year.

When we arrived at Ulldecona I was not forry to find that my guide intended to pafs through it; for it is a moft miferable village. Yet, miferable as it is, it is inclofed by walls, and maintains two convents. At the diftance of feven hours from Benicarlo we took up our lodging at a venta.

All the mountains on our left, whilft we were travelling by the margin of the fea, and all thofe we traverfed, when paffing more inland, are of limeftone, from the neighbourhood of Morviedro to Tortofa. On thefe I noticed, as we approached the diftrict of Tortofa, many monumental croffes; but not one of thefe was of a recent date.

The

The Huerta of Tortofa is moſt delightful. Far as the eye can reach, you look down upon a plain covered with vines, olives, figs, pomegranates, apricots, mulberries, and all kinds of grain; and through this fertile vale you trace the meanderings of the Ebro, which is here wide and navigable.

Tortofa, venerable for its antiquity, now contains ten thouſand ſeven hundred and eight inhabitants, with ten convents, and five pariſh churches.

The cathedral is near the river, built under the protection of a caſtle. The front is Ionic, with maſſive pillars, ſome of which are of ſingle ſtones, as are all thoſe in the chapel of N. Señora de la Cinta. The whole edifice is void of taſte, and the interior is loaded with prepoſterous ornaments.

In the cloiſter I took notice of a chapel, which carries marks of the moſt remote antiquity, with two little columns of porphyry, the one red, the other green, which look as if they had been made before the flood. The cuſtodia of ſolid ſilver, weighing fourteen arrobas, although not ſo ancient,

cient, is more to be admired for age than for the beauty of its workmanship.

The bishop has a revenue of forty thousand ducats, or nearly four thousand four hundred pounds per annum. Twelve dignitaries have each from a thousand to fifteen hundred pounds a year. Nineteen canons receive each a thousand pesos, or one hundred and fifty pounds. Beside these, for the service of the cathedral, they have thirty-four prebendaries and minor canons, and forty chaplains.

The *funda*, or hotel, furnished in a stile superior to what I had expected, and much beyond the ventas and posadas I had lately seen, appeared comfortable at least, if not to be admired for its elegance. The landlord, an Italian, had the air and manners of an inn-keeper in France. He furnished the dinner, and set the dishes on the table. First he brought in soup, then a bouilli of bull beef; after that a fricassee of garlic and liver, followed by what he called a fricandeau; then, by way of *rôti*, a shoulder of lamb, or rather the bones covered with a skin, for I could discover no flesh upon the bones. These dishes were followed by
sallad,

sallad, and a dessert of apricots and almonds. After I had tasted the fricassee, when he introduced the subsequent dishes, he exclaimed with an air of triumph, " *Allons, courage, monsieur;*" and after all, with a tone of the highest satisfaction, " *Eh bien, avez vous bien diné?*" I could not do less than answer, " *Le mieux du monde.*"

The maid servant, who waited at table, was no less remarkable than the master in her way. She was a *gitana*, or gipsy, pretty, and elegantly made, with black hair, black eyes, and much animation in her countenance. Exceedingly attentive and alert, she moved like the wind to bring plates, supply wine and water, and, with a napkin, to keep off innumerable flies. The wine, to cool it, had been immersed in water; but when the bottle was more than half exhausted, it began to float. Seeing this, the girl, with wonderful simplicity, made repeated efforts to sink it in the water; and when she found it still persisting to emerge, she betrayed strongly, disappointment and surprise.

Gipsies are very numerous on the southern and eastern coasts of Spain; but I never saw them strolling as with us in England. I learn from Count Campomanes, that they amounted to more than ten thousand, when, in the preceding reign, they were seized in one day, and confined to prisons. Government soon grew weary of maintaining such a multitude in idleness, and discharged them all. Yet their capture, with subsequent regulations, had this good effect, that they no longer wandered in companies as beggars, nor frequented, as usual, the deserted forests, to live by robbery and plunder.

At the time when they were taken into custody, many industrious families, by the abuse of the royal edict, and under pretence that they descended from parents who had been of the gipsy race, were plundered, and reduced to poverty, without redress.

When we left Tortosa, we proceeded for two leagues along the Huerta, then ascending through the gorges of the mountains, instead of a rich valley, highly cultivated, and productive of every thing useful to the human race, we saw nothing for nine long leagues but dreary mountains, desolate and waste, covered only with palmito,

mito, cofcoja, and a few other vegetables, all ftunted in their growth.

The road is execrable; but as the rock is moftly bare, I had, from time to time, occafion to obferve fome bivalve, or extraneous foffil, in the limeftone. Succeeding travellers will find a more comfortable route by a new road now making nearer to the fea, fhorter by many miles, and almoft level, as far as Tarragona.

Among the mountains, in one little cultivated fpot, is a miferable village, called *Perello*, which was formerly a defenced city. There we took up our lodging for the night. Looking down from thence, the country before us appeared to be a wide extended plain, furrounded by high mountains, excepting to the eaft, where it is open to the fea; but as we defcended, we difcovered pointed hills innumerable, with deep ravins, and contracted vallies. At the diftance of five leagues from Perello, having climbed a fteep afcent, under the cannon of a ftrong fort, which is built on the fummit of a rock, we defcended to a venta near the fea, called *Hofpitalet*.

The plough here differs from thofe I have

have remarked in other parts of Spain: it has neither coulter, fin, nor mouldboard, nor yet wooded pins to supply that defect; but inftead of thefe, the tail of the fhare is divided, fo as to perform the fame operation as the heel and ground wrift of our ploughs. The retch is divided to ferve the purpofe of a mortice, and receive the handle; and as the tillage is with one mule, the beam terminates in fhafts.

At the diftance of a league from Hofpitalet we entered a rich plain, bounded to the left by mountains, but on the right open to the fea; and for many leagues we travelled through one continued garden, occupied by numerous villages, the lofty towers of whofe churches, to the eaft of us, reflected the rays of the fetting fun. This fertile vale, called Campo de Tarragona, produces in quick fucceffion, wheat, barley, maize, beans, peas, garvanzos, French-beans, leeks, onions, garlic, melons, cucumbers, and calabafh, artichokes, olives, oil, wine, almonds, pomegranates, figs, apricots, algarrobos, flax, hemp, filk, alfalfa, and a variety of herbs, fome for fodder, others for the fervice of the table.

Near

Near to Tarragona the olive trees were cut down to make room for vines, at a time when brandy happened to be in great requeſt, and ſince the price of that commodity has fallen, the olive yards have not been as yet renewed.

Tarragona, of all the cities in Spain, would give the moſt agreeable employment to the antiquarian. Here he would admire the remains of an amphitheatre, of a theatre, of a circus, of the palace of Auguſtus, of temples, and of an extenſive aqueduct, with fortifications, which, although of a more recent date, are ancient. The aqueduct brings water to the city from the diſtance of ſeven leagues, and croſſes a deep ravin over a bridge which is ſeven hundred feet long, and one hundred high, with eleven arches below, and twenty-five above. It was repaired at the ſole expence of the late archbiſhop.

The cathedral, a maſſive pile, was built A. D. 1117, and is therefore venerable for antiquity; but in the interior, one chapel only, dedicated to Santa Tecla, is worthy of attention. In this the dome and columns are moſt beautiful, and ſerve to ſhew what valuable marbles are to be procured in this vicinity.

The archbishop enjoys a revenue of about four thousand pounds a year. Twelve dignitaries, twenty-four canons, as many minor canons, and forty chaplains, are well provided for at present, and will in future have increasing incomes; because the king means to reduce their number, as vacancies occur, and add considerably to the revenue of the survivors; improving at the same time, and in the same proportion, the royal third.

Nothing can be more politic than this measure; for thus quietly, and without clamour, the useless wealth of the cathedrals will be restored to the community, and gradually relieve the distresses of the state. Whenever the critical moment shall arrive, eleven convents at Tarragona will contribute their lands and treasures to the necessities of a sinking nation.

This city contains seven thousand five hundred souls at present; but whenever the canal of Arragon shall be navigable, the whole country will feel the influence of reviving

viving commerce; and, among other cities, this may regain its ancient population.

The trade of this city is now confined to wine and brandy; but for home confumption they carry on a confiderable fifhery.

To protect the inhabitants from the incurfions of the Moors, they have erected batteries. Thefe are the more needful, becaufe the ancient fortifications are gone to ruin, and the Algerines have committed frequent depredations on this coaft. Spain, indeed, has lately concluded a treaty with Algiers, but no one can conjecture how long the peace will laft.

Beef is fold for twenty-one quartos the double pound of thirty-fix ounces, or about two pence halfpenny our pound.

Mutton is worth thirty-four, or about four pence farthing.

June 27, leaving Tarragona, we paffed over an extenfive beach, covered with fifhermen and nets; then, quitting the feafhore, we traverfed a well cultivated plain, found refrefhment at Figretta, beyond which the road goes under a Roman arch, and at night we took up our lodging at Monjus.

In

In the way, I took notice that the land is chiefly tilled with cows, and admired every where the patient and laborious peasant unremittingly employed in the cultivation of his land, even when expofed to the full ftroke of the mid-day fun.

Near to the numerous villages through which we paffed, I was delighted to obferve the rich abundance of corn, olives, vines, figs, almonds, mulberries, and complete hedges of pomegranate, now covered with its fcarlet bloffom.

As we proceeded, we difcovered Montferrat, which at firft appeared juft rifing up in the horizon, and almoft loft in clouds; but as we advanced, we could more diftinctly trace it ftretching in the wide expanfe, and bounding an extenfive plain.

When we arrived at *Monjus*, the old man, who was mafter of the pofada, was winnowing his wheat, after having trodden it on the area with his cattle. His firft operation was to get out the ftraw by means of rakes; then he toffed the grain with a four pronged fork, in order to expofe it to the wind. Having thus cleared it from the chaff, he sifted it, then shogged it in closer sieves to separate the lighter seeds; yet, after all his pains and labour, I observed among his wheat, barley, oats, vetches of various species, cockle (agrostemma githaco) with other ponderous seeds, small gravel, and little clods of earth, such as we always find in wheat imported from every part of Spain.

What a pity is it, that in most of our counties, and in every part of France and Spain, farmers should be unacquainted with the winnowing machine, which, imported first from Holland, is used all over Scotland, and countenanced by our respectable Society of Arts! a drawing and description of this excellent machine, published by the Society in London, is highly worthy of attention, as being the only one by which any species of grain can be properly cleansed; I will not merely say for seed, but even for the market.

About Monjus, I took notice that all the corn, for want of carts, of waggons, and of cars, was brought home, not as in Devonshire and Cornwall, in bundles,
hanging

hanging against the horse's sides, but disposed on a square frame, and fastened on his back.

June 28. Having passed *Villa franca de Panades*, we had the satisfaction, once more, to travel on good roads, well formed and made, at a vast expence, through rocks, and over the deepest ravins, or the gorges of high mountains. Some of the bridges designed to form a junction between these, are most stupendous, and shew clearly the enterprising spirit of this laborious nation.

In many of their deepest cuts through the interposing rock, I took occasion to observe the strata. They are generally limestone, and incline more so towards the sea; but as I approached the Lobregat, I remarked, at a very considerable depth, thin strata of schist interposed between those of limestone.

The prospects in this part of Catalonia are most enchanting, and change at every step. Mountains are seen peeping over mountains, and the hills assume a pleasing variety of forms. Many are shaded with thick woods, many with luxuriant crops of

corn,

corn, and not a few lift up their rugged cliffs above the reſt, and hide their heads among the clouds. Induſtry climbs among theſe rocks, and every ſpot where the plough can go, or the vine can fix its roots, is made productive, and abounds with either corn, or wine, or oil. In the vallies we ſee the peaſants engaged in tillage, and with two ſtrong oxen breaking up their fallows; where, by means of a coulter and a mould-board to a well conſtructed plough, they turn deep furrows, ſuch as I had never before remarked in Spain.

As we approach Barcelona, all is in motion, and the whole road appears alive, with horſes, mules, waggons, carts, and people, thronging to the market with their wares. No ſuch activity, no ſuch appearance of buſineſs is ſeen in any other of the provinces.

At ſix in the evening we arrived, and I had the happineſs of meeting my valuable friend the conſul in good health.

Between Valencia and Barcelona, the poſadas are tolerably good, but dear, when compared with other parts of Spain, ex-

cepting

cepting only for the carriers. Thefe pay twenty quartos, or lefs than fix pence, for their fupper, and have plenty of every thing, fifh, butcher's meat, poultry, and good wine, with bread and garden ftuff; but to a traveller every article is charged, and his bill feldom amounts to lefs than thirty reals.

RETURN TO BARCELONA.

IMMEDIATELY on my return to Barcelona, I paid my refpects to the count of Afalto, captain general of the province, and governor of the city, with a letter from count Florida Blanca, which alone was fufficient to infure me an agreeable reception. This gentleman, diftinguifhed for politenefs, fhewed me all poffible attention, gave me the information I defired, and readily granted the only requeft I had occafion to make.

Through him I had the honour of being introduced to the bifhop of the diocefe, don Guvino de Valladares y Mesía. I was the more folicitous for this honour, becaufe the good prelate had been reprefented as a bigot, whofe fole employment was to count his beads, and his only paffion to live fecluded

cluded from the world. My friends had assured me, that, as a protestant, I had no chance of being well received, and that, if from attention to the count, he should be inclined to shew civility, I should be disgusted with his coldness. At all events I was resolved to see him, and I am happy that I did; for I not only found him easy of access, and more than commonly conversable, but so far removed from bigotry, that, before I quitted him, he pressed me to return, and to stay some days with him.

His residence is two leagues from Barcelona, a little to the westward of Mongat, on a gentle declivity, open to the meridian sun, and looking down upon the sea.

The party with me on this visit consisted of the grand vicar, and my friend don Nicolas Lasso the inquisitor. At the bishop's I had the happiness of meeting don Tomas de Lorenzana, who is brother to the archbishop of Toledo, and himself bishop of Gerona.

The meeting of two prelates is a phœnomenon in Spain, because the moment a minister of the altar accepts a mitre, he devotes his life wholly to the duties of his office,

office, confines himself altogether to his diocefe, and is loft both to his friends and to his family. On the prefent occafion, therefore, the vifit of this prelate was neither in the way of ceremony nor of friendfhip, but to affift in the dedication of a temple.

I was much pleafed with my vifit, and flattered by the attention of thefe venerable men. They differ exceedingly in character, yet each appeared amiable in his way. The bifhop of Gerona, although advanced in years, is lively and volatile, full of wit and humour. The bifhop of Barcelona is placid and grave, yet pleafant and agreeable, and peculiary diftinguifhed for benevolence, fond of retirement, and much attached to books. He entertained us well, and feemed pleafed with this little interruption to his ftudies. To me, his invitation to repeat my vifit appeared fo cordial, and his converfation fo engaging, that I was mortified in not being able to prolong my ftay. In the evening we returned, as we had come, in his coach and fix to Barcelona.

Having now fo good an opportunity to gain information, I made enquiries refpecting

ing the population of Catalonia, the taxes impofed on the inhabitants, and the revenue derived to the community from this induſtrious province.

In the beginning of the prefent century they reckoned one hundred and one thoufand nine hundred and eighty-fix houfes, and only three hundred and ninety-one thoufand four hundred and ninety inhabitants; but then, it muſt be remembered, that the province had been ravaged by civil war. The houfes remained, but many of the inhabitants had vaniſhed. In the year 1768, when the biſhops gave an account of the population, each in his diocefe, they made the fubfequent return: men, one hundred and eighty-nine thoufand two hundred and fifty-two; women, one hundred and ninety-two thoufand feven hundred and fixty-three; boys, three hundred and thirteen thoufand and feventy-nine; girls, three hundred and twenty thoufand nine hundred and fixteen; clergy, regular and fecular, fourteen thoufand two hundred and thirty-five. In all, one million and thirty thoufand two hundred and forty-five.

Since that period it is allowed that the
population

population is not diminished; yet, in the last returns to government, dated A. D. 1787, and published by authority, we find only eight hundred and one thousand six hundred and two inhabitants. Of these, six thousand nine hundred and eighty-three are under vows, and one thousand two hundred and sixty-six are knights. Now, the difference between these returns being more than two hundred and twenty-eight thousand in favour of the former, when no cause for such a deficiency in the latter can be assigned, evidently marks some error in one or both of them; and, indeed, I have it from the best authority, that these accounts, notwithstanding the most watchful attention on the part of government, always come short, and very short, of the actual population, because it is the interest of every family, parish, and district, to conceal their numbers, in order to avoid the capitation tax.

Catalonia enjoys the privilege of exemption from the alcavala, cientos, and millones; in lieu of which they pay ten per cent. on all rents, whether belonging to individuals

dividuals or communities, fuch as, of houfes, lands, tithes, mills, public houfes, and public ovens, with ten per cent. on the fuppofed gains of merchants, and mechanics. Labourers pay eight and one-third per cent. fuppofing them to work a hundred days in the year, at three reals a day. Artifts and manufacturers contribute in the fame proportion annually for a hundred and eighty days. Oxen, cows and calves, horfes, mules, fheep and lambs, with pigs, and other animals, if of the larger fpecies, pay three reals each per annum; thofe of the middling fize, one and an half; and the fmalleft, one-third of a real; always fuppofing the reals to be ardites, of which fourteen are equal to fifteen and two-thirty-fourth reals vellon.

The produce of thefe taxes amounted, A. D. 1721, as ftated by Uftariz, to twelve million eight hundred and feventy thoufand feven hundred and feventy-four reals vellon, or one hundred and twenty-eight thoufand pounds fterling, and were as follows:

The

	Reals Vellon.
The lands at ten per cent. making allowance for unfruitful years	5,346,341
Tithes received by private people of the laity	159,021
Houses, in proportion to the rent	700,956
Emoluments of communities	256,706
Mills	83,978
Quit rents	308,608
Personal labour	3,099,854
Cattle	249,193
Commerce	175,000
	10,379,657
This falling short of what was expected, the same year was added in due proportion	2,491,117
Total reals vellon	12,870,774
Beside the above, Catalonia paid a composition in lieu of lodging, straw, light wood, and utensils for the troops	4,500,000
Rent of tobacco, salt, the customs, posts, stamps, crusades, subsidy, and excusado	30,000,000

Royal

Royal patrimony	560,718
Rent of snow	35,420
Lottery	219,818
Total reals vellon	48,186,730

Thus the whole amount of the taxes collected in Catalonia was, A. D. 1721, four hundred and eighty-one thousand eight hundred and sixty-seven pounds sterling. But as the revenue of Spain is more than doubled since that period, should we allow the same increase for Catalonia, we must state the revenue arising from this province at little less than a million sterling, which, according to the computed population, is twenty shillings annually for each person; whereas, taking the whole peninsula together, the Spaniards pay no more than ten shillings each per annum.

This contribution is relatively heavy; yet, considering the peculiar advantages and resources of the Catalans, it is comparatively light; for being freed from the stagnating influence of the alcavala, cientos, and millones, they enjoy a decided superiority

rity over provinces which have never claimed the same indulgence. Unfettered by these impolitic restraints, their industry is free, whilst that of less-favoured provinces, harassed incessantly by the collectors of the revenue, is crippled in all its operations.

In addition to these immunities, as it has been well remarked, the great number of troops constantly quartered in Catalonia not only gives to the farmers and manufacturers a ready market for their commodities, but contributes much to maintain good order in the province. For near two centuries previous to the accession of the present family, Catalonia was infested with banditti, who, by robbing and plundering passengers, interrupted the safe and easy communication of the cities with each other, and prevented, in a great measure, the interior commerce of the country. But when Philip V. after a severe conflict, had obtained the sceptre, considering the strong attachment the Catalans discovered for his rival, to prevent insurrections, he stationed a considerable detachment of his troops in this doubtful part of his dominions. The immediate consequence of this provision was the reftoration of good order; the fubfequent effect has been the revival of commerce, by a quick and certain demand for all the productions of their induftry. (v. Campomanes Induftria Popular, p. 72.)

It is peculiarly fortunate for Catalonia, that the popular prejudice is favourable to commerce; for here artifts and manufacturers are as much honoured and refpected as in other provinces they are defpifed and treated with contempt.

But that, which contributes moft to the wealth and profperity of Catalonia, is the power which gentlemen of landed property have over their eftates, to grant a particular fpecies of leafe called *Eftablifhment by Emfiteutic Contracts*. To that circumftance Count Campomanes pays particular attention, when he would account for the fuperior cultivation and improvement of this induftrious province; nor is he fingular in his opinion. He not only obferves, refpecting Catalonia, *El ufu del derecho emfiteutico mantiene alli al labrador fobre fuftierras y produce un fobrante de gentes para los oficios*; but to form the contraft he remarks, that Andalufia, although more fertile

fertile than either Catalonia or Galicia, yet is deftitute of induftry, becaufe the land being occupied by few proprietors, the bulk of the people are day labourers, who only find occafional employment. Hence, clothed in rags and wretchednefs, they crowd into cities, where they obtain a precarious livelihood through the bounty of rich ecclefiaftics. (Camp. E. P. Ap. 3. p. cxlix. and I. P. 73.)

Not merely in Andalufia, but in other provinces, the great eftates being ftrictly entailed, and adminiftered on the proprietor's account, little land is to be rented by the farmer, lefs can be purchafed by the monied man, and, for want of floating property, induftry is left to languifh. In Catalonia it is totally the reverfe of this.

By the *Emfiteutic contract*, the great proprietor inheriting more land than he can cultivate to profit, has power to grant any given quantity for a term of years, either abfolute or conditional, either for lives, or in perpetuity, always referving a quit-rent, like our copyholds, with a relief on every fucceffion, a fine on the alienation of the land, and other feignioral rights dependant on the cuftom custom of the district, such as tithes, mills, public-houses, the obligation to plough his land, to furnish him with teams, and to pay hearth-money, with other contributions, by way of commutation for ancient stipulated services.

One species of grant for uncultivated land, to be planted with vines, admitted formerly of much dispute. The tenant, holding his land as long as the first planted vines should continue to bear fruit, in order to prolong this term, was accustomed to train layers from the original stocks, and, by metaphysical distinctions between identity and diversity, to plead, that the first planted vines were not exhausted; claiming thus the inheritance in perpetuity. After various litigations and inconsistent decisions of the judges, it was finally determined, that this species of grant should convey a right to the possession for fifty years, unless the plantation itself should previously fail.

The lord of this allodial property may appoint any one as judge, with the assistance of an attorney, to hold court for him, provided he has previously obtained permission from the provincial court, or, supposing the district

diſtrict to be a barony, from the baron or his ordinary judge. Having conſtituted the tribunal, the lord, even whilſt a cauſe is pending, may at pleaſure remove the judge, and name another in his place, and the tenant has, at any period of the trial, a right to his challenge, without aſſigning reaſons, other than his own ſuſpicions. Each party may equally reject three advocates appointed for aſſeſſors.

The reſerved rent is paid commonly in money; but often the agreement is for oil, wine, corn, or poultry.

Should the property thus granted in fee paſs into mortmain, the lord of the ſoil may inſiſt on its being ſold, or he may increaſe the reſerved rent in proportion to the value of the uſual fine.

The tenant, whenever ſummoned, muſt produce in court his title, which he is bound to trace upward, till it arrives ultimately at the royal grant; and when his term expires, on quitting, he muſt be paid for his improvements, before he can be legally ejected: but at the ſame time he may be compelled to indemnify his lord for all damages ſuſtained by his neglect.

Should the tenant be defirous of quitting before the expiration of his term, he is at liberty to do it; but in that cafe he is precluded from all claims for his improvements.

The tenure in Catalonia is evidently feodal. All property in land is traced up to the king, and is held by knights fervice from the crown, fubject to relief, to fines, and to efcheat. Under the royal grant, the great lords claim, not merely tithes of all lands not being freehold, with quit rents and fines, mills, and public houfes, as we have remarked above, but the right of appointing magiftrates and receiving tolls on the paffage of cattle over their eftates.

To the power retained by them of making emfiteutic contracts, has with reafon been attributed the cultivation of fuch wafte lands as are moft fufceptible of tillage, and the confequent increafe of population. Induftry has been promoted, new families have been called into exiftence, and many, refcued from poverty and wretchednefs, are now maintained in comfortable affluence. In the year 1738, one James Vilaplana purchafed at a public auction, for

two

two hundred livres Catalan, a tract of waste land, on which, in 1778, were found twenty families established, although he had reserved one third of this possession for himself; and the whole being planted with vines, for which the soil was best adapted, what had been originally purchased for two hundred livres became, in the space of forty years, worth many thousands.

Yet advantageous as this kind of establishment has been, both to individuals and to the community at large, some great proprietors are so inattentive, both to the general good and to their private benefit, that they leave their lands uncultivated. Even in Catalonia, according to the government returns, more than three hundred villages have been deserted.

On my return to Barcelona, recommended by the minister to the protection of the governor, feeling myself strong, I ventured to inquire more freely (than I had before thought prudent) into the conduct of the inquisition. In my former visit I had cultivated friendship with the inquisitors, yet I had always approached them with a degree of reverential awe; but now I questioned

tioned them without reserve or fear. The point at which I laboured was to converse with some who were confined, and understanding that Mr. Howard had visited their prisons, I pleaded for the same indulgence. To this request they answered, that I was certainly mistaken; for that no human being, unless in custody, or himself an officer of the inquisition, could be admitted to see the interior of their prisons; but they assured me in the most solemn manner, that the prisoners were not merely treated with humanity, but enjoyed every possible indulgence. The apartments, in which they are confined are spacious, airy, clean, and commodious. They are permitted to send for their own bed, with books, pen, ink, and paper. They have their own provisions, and if they are poor, they are well fed and comfortably lodged at the expence of the inquisitors. The alcalde waits upon them four times a day to receive their orders, and once a fortnight one of the inquisitors visits every apartment to see that all is in good condition, and to inquire if the prisoners are treated with humanity.

To provide funds for the expence of this
tribunal,

tribunal, they confiscate the goods of all, who are condemned.

Neither their superior officers, nor yet their familiars, or lowest servants and messengers, are amenable before the civil courts, nor accountable for their crimes and offences to any but their own tribunal.

My friends, the inquisitors of Barcelona, felt exceedingly sore about the trial of the beggar at Madrid; and assured me, that the only reason why the king required the inquisition to take cognizance of so contemptible a wretch was out of tenderness to the many ladies of high fashion, whose names must have appeared, had the prosecution been conducted in the civil courts. They likewise gave me to understand, that as long as the priesthood should be debarred from marriage, and confessors continue liable to abuse the confidence reposed in them, the secrecy, the prudence, and, when needful, the severity of the inquisition, would be the only effectual restraint against licentiousness and the universal depravation of their morals.

When a prisoner is discharged, the inquisitors exact an oath of secrecy, and
should

should this be violated, the offender would have reason to repent his rashness; for, taken from his family in the middle of the night, he might never be released again.

The dread of this imposes silence on all who have been once confined. The Dutch consul now at Barcelona, through the long period of five and thirty years, has never been prevailed upon to give any account of his confinement, and appears to be much agitated whenever urged to relate in what manner he was treated. His fellow sufferer, M. Falconet, then a boy, turned grey during the short space of his confinement, and to the day of his death, although retired to Montpellier, observed the most tenacious silence on the subject. His sole offence had been destroying a picture of the blessed Virgin; and his friend, the Dutch consul, being present on that occasion, and not having turned accuser, was considered as a partner in his guilt.

For my own part, I am inclined to think, that in proportion as light has been diffused in Europe, even inquisitors have learnt humanity. But facts speaking so strongly for themselves, we must continue

to

to lament that darkness should so far prevail as to leave the least vestige of inquisitorial power; for, wherever it exists, it must be liable to abuse, and clemency must be merely accidental.

During the whole week immediately preceding my final departure from the city, all the world was occupied with festivity on account of the beatification of two saints lately received into the calendar. Philip IV. and Philip V. had, for this purpose, exerted all their influence, promoting contributions to defray the expence of the process at the court of Rome, and urging the most powerful arguments with his holiness the Pope; but all their arguments were vain, till the general voice, and the more powerful interest of Charles III. prevailed.

The citizens, on this occasion, gave full scope to the expressions of their joy. In the convent of S. Francisco de Paula, to which order the new saints belong, they had service every evening, accompanied with a strong band of music, both vocal and instrumental. These reverend fathers, in the ardour of their zeal, had cut down their

their orange grove to make room for a model of Monjuich. Not far from thence, one of the faints, S. Bono, was reprefented as a foldier, with a company of horfe, climbing a fteep afcent, and ready to tumble over a wall into a well, whilft San Francifco was attending to deliver him. After this miraculous efcape, the foldier became a faint, and embraced the order of his patron. The only miracles afcribed to him, whilft living, were his detecting a boy, who was ftealing artichokes from the garden of his convent, and a friar, who was tempted by fome fifh to incur the guilt of facrilege. But now, after the lapfe of two hundred and thirty years, he is become the patron of women in child-birth, and his relics are faid to cure all difeafes.

The ftreets in the vicinity of the convent, and nearly over one quarter of the city, were illuminated every night; the houfes were covered with white linen, and the balconies, adorned with looking glafs, reflected light from innumerable tapers. The fhops, fitted up like facred grottos, had each its altar, and many elegant chapels were conftructed in the middle of the ftreets.

All the narrow lanes, dressed with green branches so as to resemble groves, were hung with festoons of flowers, intermixed with coloured lamps. Many of the principal inhabitants had music in their houses; and every evening, till near midnight, thousands were crowding through the streets to hear and see the united efforts of all ranks to honour the memory of their countrymen, now received among the saints.

During my residence at Barcelona, I had the happiness of cultivating an acquaintance with two very ingenious physicians, Don Francisco Sanponts, and Don Francisco Salva. I found them well acquainted with the writings of the best nosologists, and expert in the improvements of modern chemistry. With one of their experiments, then new to me, I was peculiarly delighted. I had seen Dr. Priestley produce dephlogisticated air from manganese in great abundance, and more sparingly from vegetables exposed to the meridian sun; but these gentlemen, by a similar process, obtained, in the space of a few hours, from a small portion of American aloe *(agave Americana)* half a pint of vital, or dephlogisticated air; and at the fame time affured me, that from no vegetable fubftance had they ever been able to procure an equal quantity in proportion to the furface expofed to the folar rays. Having extracted and transferred this to a phial, in it they immerged a twifted iron wire, with a fmall portion of amadou at the end, which having kindled into flame they had previoufly extinguifhed. Inftantly this fmoking tinder blazed, and the iron burned, like nitre, with a moft vivid flame, cafting off little ftars of light, and leaving at laft a number of fmall fhot, perfectly rotund, which were nothing but the fcoria of the iron. A fimilar portion of the leaf, when the day was cloudy, produced fixed air, which fpeedily extinguifhed flame; but the quantity obtained in the fpace of a few hours was not confiderable. For thefe beautiful experiments they are indebted to Dr. Ingen-Houfz.

Of threefcore phyficians fettled at Barcelona, thefe two are the moft diftinguifhed, and have the moft extenfive practice. One of them favoured me with a fight of his lift. He had vifited more than forty patients in the morning, and he was to fee as many before he went to bed. Among thefe were many merchants, manufacturers, and officers; yet he did not expect to receive a hundred reals, that is twenty fhillings, for the whole practice of the day.

Although not rich, they had occafion, a few years fince, to fhew a high and independent fpirit, for which they deferve the higheft commendation. When General O'Neille was governor, (A. D. 1784,) the putrid fever, already mentioned more than once, raged in Catalonia, as in Arragon and other provinces of Spain. The phyficians, fummoned by the governor, like thofe of Carthagena, were required to engage, that from thenceforth they would prefcribe no medicine befide the famous opiate recommended by Dr. Mafdevall. Not fatisfied with this, the governor had prepared a certificate, fimilar to the one produced at Carthagena, for them to fign. The doctors Salva and Sanponts, in the name of all the reft, remonftrated; but could obtain no other anfwer, than that the king would have it fo, and that the prifon doors ftood open to receive them. Our chieftains, however, not to be intimidated, continuing firm to their refolution, and being well fupported by their corps, at laft came off triumphant, and were permitted to prefcribe whatever medicines they thought proper. The general, although as a foldier he had been accuftomed to obedience, yet being gentle and difcreet, he chofe rather to report the matter to the court, than at once to carry his threats into execution. Here the matter refted.

Dr. Mafdevall, in his publication, claims the invention of this opiate, and reprefents it not merely as a fpecific in putrid fevers, but as a panacea, infallible in all kinds of fever, and a fovereign remedy in every difeafe incident to the human frame. But as the phyficians of Barcelona were by no means fatisfied of this, they refifted his pretenfions; and as fome of them had noticed this famous opiate in the *Journal de Medecine*, fo far back as A. D. 1769, they denied him the merit of invention. In reality, this formula was known and defcribed under the appellation of Boucher's opiate, and the nature of the decompofition taking place on the admixture of the

various

various articles was well deſcribed in the Journal of 1778.

The mixture of tartar emetic with the Peruvian bark has been a favourite medicine in France. In the year 1779, the Royal Medical Society at Paris, in their Memoirs, p. 249, recommended highly a drachm of the former, with an ounce of the latter, to be uſed in putrid fevers; and at Barcelona they were already in the habit of combining tartar emetic, cremor tartari, and Peruvian bark, before ever they received the royal mandate.

In converſing with theſe phyſicians, I was ſtruck with the number of lunatics under confinement in the ſeveral provinces of Spain; and when I returned to England, I compared their account of Catalonia with the government returns. By theſe it appears, that in Arragon the number is two hundred and forty-four; in Catalonia, one hundred and fourteen; in Valencia, one hundred and twenty-one; in Andaluſia, ninety-nine; in Granada, forty-one; in Toledo, forty-two; in the province of Leon, two; and in Avila, one. In the other interior provinces no mention is made of any.

Thus stands the fact; but as for the foundation of this difference between the maritime and the inland provinces in this respect, neither they nor any one with whom I have conversed on the subject, could suggest any thing worthy of remark. I have, therefore, been contented simply to state the fact, and leave it as I found it.

Before I quitted Catalonia, I wished to have visited some of the numerous mines among the mountains; but could never find a convenient opportunity. I was, however, favoured with a copy of the schedule, containing a minute account of all the mines discovered in the province, drawn up for the use of government by the servants of the crown.

From this it appears, that although minerals have yielded hitherto little to the revenue, and not much to individuals, they have numerous mines of antimony, iron, lead, copper, silver, with one of gold, and many of coal. Some of these are too remote from water carriage, others cannot be worked to profit for want of timber. But that which is most remarkable is, that two private adventurers, Don Joseph Solanell,

of

of Ripoll, and one Canadell, a merchant of Berga, having obtained a grant from the crown, undertook to work fourteen coal mines in various and distant parishes; when, to open any one effectually, would require not merely skilful miners, but a weight of capital, such as few individuals in Spain can be supposed to command. Coals are chiefly found in the district of *Villa-franca*; silver and copper abound in the *valle de Aràn*; but coal, silver, and gold, have all been discovered in the vicinity of Lerida.

It is certainly for the happiness of this principality, that the mines are not made more productive. In mining countries, the gains are exceedingly uncertain; a gambling spirit is encouraged, agriculture is neglected, and poverty prevails. If the mineral is raised on the adventurers account, unless they discover uncommon treasures, they will be inevitably ruined. If the working miners become sub-adventurers, they either gain too little, and are wretched; or they get too much, and soon contract strong habits of indolence, prodigality, and vice.

Of this truth we have a melancholy
proof

proof at home. Let any one pass through the county, which most abounds with mines, and in the mining parishes he will be struck, every moment, with the sight of poverty and wretchedness. Seeing multitudes lost to the community, as to all useful purposes, and abandoned to misery, he will enquire, if no provision has been made to relieve the distresses of the poor? The result of his enquiries will be simply this; that in circumstances similar to theirs, no laws, either human or divine, restrain the uncultivated mind from vice; and that the most liberal contributions of the rich only tend to increase the wants and the distresses of the poor. He will hear, to his astonishment, that in some places the whole landed property is absorbed and lost in the vain attempt of relieving poverty; and that they, among the poor, whose gains have been the greatest, are universally the most distressed. In the districts where mines have not been ever heard of, and where all are engaged in the cultivation of the soil, he will admire the prevalence of industry, sobriety, and virtue; he will be charmed with simplicity of manners; he will find

fewer

fewer objects of distress; and, upon enquiry he will learn, that little is required from the hand of charity to relieve the poor.

Some individuals have gained wealth by mines, but not the community, because the blanks are more in number than the prizes. However, therefore, the hope of gain may influence the individual to such bold and hazardous adventures, a prudent sovereign will rather encourage his subjects to prefer the more slow and certain, the moderate, **yet regular and healthful** gains of agriculture. The spirit of mining should be the last to meet encouragement; yet in Spain it appears to be among the first. If agriculture were carried to the utmost possible extent; if the lands now desolate and waste were reduced to tillage; if all the vallies susceptible of that improvement were supplied with water; if the projected canals and the high roads were finished; if neither agriculture, manufactures, nor commerce could find employment for their people and their capitals; it might then, and not till then, become a question, whether the surplus of their population should find vent in emigrations, or whether

ther they should look for antimony, cobalt, bismuth, mercury, lead, copper, silver, and gold, at home.

Before I quitted Barcelona I had a curious paper put into my hands, which made me wish for the one corresponding to it. This was a schedule, with enquiries directed, A. D. 1575, to all the prelates and corregidors, by Philip II; but I could not learn what answers had been returned, or what steps taken in consequence, of these inquiries.

Among the fifty-seven heads, on which the corregidors were to make report, the major part related to geography, and the local situation of each village; to natural and civil history; to remarkable characters, both ancient and modern; to heraldry; to the municipal government, and state of defence; to agriculture, and the productions of each district; to mineralogy, with a special reference to gold, silver, iron, copper, lead, mercury, or other metals, but without any mention of coal, of which they appear not to have had the least idea.

Of the remaining queries the subsequent are the most remarkable:

1st,

1st, What is the present number of houses and families? Were they formerly more numerous? If so, To what cause must be attributed the subsequent diminution?

2d, Are all the inhabitants employed in useful labour? How many are knights, and what immunities do these enjoy?

3d, What entailed estates are there?

4th, Are the people prosperous and flourishing? What manufactures do they carry on? In what do they excel?

5th, What waste lands and commons have they? What is the value of these to the community? What do they collect for the passage of goods and of cattle through their territories?

6th, What privileges and immunities do they enjoy, and what special customs do they plead? For what reasons were these granted?

7th, Supposing the town to be under the jurisdiction of a lord, what emoluments, privileges, or pre-eminence, does he, or any other person, derive from it?

8th, What is the value of the tithes, and to whom do they belong?

9th,

9th, In cities and collegiate churches, what is the value of the various benefices?

10th, What is the value of the bishopric, and of all the livings in the diocese?

11th, What convents for monks, for nuns, and for beatas, are in your district? What are the numbers under vows? Who were the founders of these religious houses? and, What is the value of their rents?

12th, What hospitals have you, and what is their revenue?

13th, How many public houses are in the district? To whom do they belong, and what are they worth?

14th, What depopulated villages are in your district, and what was the cause of their decay?

15th, Does your town claim a vote in cortes? if not, How, and by what city is it represented there?

16th, What festivals are observed, beside those appointed by the church?

17th, What remarkable relics are in your churches, and what miracles have been performed by them?

It is evident from the general scope of these

these inquiries, that the design of Philip II. was to gain a perfect knowledge of his kingdom, with a view to political economy; but in order to dazzle the eyes of his subjects, he intermixed queries which had no reference to that subject.

Were we now in possession of the answers to these most interesting queries, we should be able to judge how far the country has been depopulated in two centuries, since the change of government, and since the discovery of America; but for want of these authentic documents, we can only know in general that the nation has suffered much, without being able to state precisely the loss which has been sustained by these unfortunate events.

Should either the present, or any succeeding monarch, gradually extend the bounds of freedom, agreeable to the principles now prevalent in Europe; should he shake off the colonies, and contract the limits of his unwieldy empire; should he banish his inquisitors, and invite foreigners of all descriptions to settle in his country; and should he bend his whole attention to cultivate the arts of peace; this most fertile kingdom

kingdom would speedily recover, without dangerous convulsions, from her wounds; would regain her former population, strength, and consequence in Europe; and, establishing her public credit on a firm foundation, would surpass, by a rapid progress, all her ancient splendor.

When the time arrived for my departure and return to England, I made an agreeable party with the consul of Barcelona, to take the rout of Switzerland, than which, for a naturalist, no country can be more interesting. In the way I paid particular attention to the strata, and to every appearance of extraneous fossils. Of this tour, should health permit, I may hereafter give a particular account, and endeavour to establish facts, such as will convince the most incredulous, that the Mosaic account of the universal deluge is strictly and literally true.

From Barcelona to Bellegarde we returned by the same way which I have described at my entrance into Spain. Arriving here at the summit of the Pyrenees, I cast one longing lingering look behind, and quitted with regret a country, where, independent of multiplied civilities and personal attentions,

attentions, for which I felt myself deeply indebted to my friends, I had been led so often to admire the boundless generosity of the inhabitants. To express all that I feel, on the recollection of their goodness, would appear like adulation; but I may venture at least to say, that simplicity, sincerity, generosity, a high sense of dignity, and strong principles of honour, are the most prominent and striking features of the Spanish character. In a word, whatever in them I have been accustomed to admire, I attribute to themselves, and to their intrinsic excellence; whatever I have blamed, must be ascribed to the accidental corruptions of their government.

Considering the similarity of character between the two nations, the Spanish and the English, with the strong predilection of the former in favour of the latter, the peculiar wants of each, and their mutual ability to supply those wants, I cannot but lament sincerely that a better understanding should not subsist between them, leading in the first instance, if not to a new family compact, at least to a family connection, and issuing finally in a commercial inter-

intercourfe equally beneficial to both nations.

Thefe are the earneft wifhes of the Spaniards, as appears by their well known adage:

> Con todo el mundo guerra
> Y paz con Ynglaterra.

"Peace with England, and war with all the world." From one end of the kingdom to the other this fentiment prevails; and fuch a ftrong defire for the union of their moft amiable prince, the infant don Antonio, with one of our princeffes, that their wifhes conftantly kindle into hope. During my abode in Spain, when at any time, as often happened, a rumour fpread that this event would fpeedily take place, being readily and univerfally believed, every eye was feen to fparkle with the joyful expectation.

In the prefent circumftances of the royal families, both in Spain and Portugal, fuch a connection would promife peculiar advantages to the princefs who fhould vifit Spain, becaufe it is more than poffible fhe might give a fovereign to them both, under whofe
fceptre

sceptre those kingdoms would for ever be united.

From such a connection no inconveniencies could arise to England, because catholics are by law excluded from our throne, and the whole system of their religion, with astonishing rapidity, is mouldering away. The papal authority is no longer to be feared. The French never owned allegiance to the see of Rome, and at the present moment, superstition in that vast empire lies prostrate in the dust, without the most distant hope of rising into power. Germany, under the dominion of Joseph and of Leopold, is become in a manner protestant, whilst catholics themselves, protesting, have made a new religious æra in our island.

Knowledge in the present day is not, as formerly, confined within the walls of Rome. Science universally prevails, and the sovereigns of Europe will never more consult the college of cardinals to settle their disputes. The times are changed, and, without pretending to more than common sagacity, we may venture to affirm, that the papal authority has received its

A a 2   mortal

mortal wound, and to predict, that superstition will never more revive. In these circumstances, the national religion has little to fear by accepting the offers, should such be made by any catholic court, of inter-marriage with our princesses, whose character, it may be said without suspicion of adulation, throughout Europe stands so high as to attract the attention of every crowned family, and whose liberal education and habits must make them eminently prove a blessing to the country where they go, tending to promote universal peace and a free commercial intercourse in Europe.

APPENDIX.

APPENDIX.

CASTILLIAN MONEY.

			Penny.
1 Maravedis is equal to	—		$\frac{9}{131}$
2 ditto	—	ditto	—	$\frac{9}{64}$
3 ditto	—	ditto	—	$\frac{27}{131}$
4 ditto	—	ditto a Quarto, or	$\frac{9}{32}$
5 ditto	—	ditto	—	$\frac{45}{131}$
6 ditto	—	ditto	—	$\frac{27}{64}$
7 ditto	—	ditto	—	$\frac{63}{131}$
8 ditto	—	ditto two Quartos, or	$\frac{9}{16}$
9 ditto	—	ditto	—	$\frac{91}{132}$
10 ditto	—	ditto	—	$\frac{45}{64}$
11 ditto	—	ditto	—	$\frac{99}{132}$
12 ditto	—	ditto three Quartos	$\frac{27}{32}$
13 ditto	—	ditto	—	$\frac{117}{131}$
14 ditto	—	ditto	—	$\frac{61}{64}$

15 Maravedis

APPENDIX.

			s.	d.
15 Maravedis is equal to	—		1	$\frac{7}{128}$
16 ditto —	ditto four Quartos		1	$\frac{1}{4}$
17 ditto —	ditto —		1	$\frac{25}{128}$
32 ditto —	ditto eight Quartos		2	$\frac{1}{2}$
34 ditto —	ditto 8 $\frac{1}{2}$ Quartos		2	$\frac{25}{64}$
64 ditto a Real of Plate equal to			4	$\frac{1}{2}$
136 ditto a Peceta ditto	—		9	$\frac{9}{16}$
1,000 ditto —	ditto —	5	10	$\frac{5}{16}$
10,000 ditto —	ditto	2 18	7	$\frac{1}{2}$

---

			s.	d.
1 Real Vellon is equal to	—	0	2	$\frac{25}{64}$
2 ditto —	ditto —	0	4	$\frac{25}{32}$
3 ditto —	ditto —	0	7	$\frac{11}{64}$
4 ditto, a Peceta, ditto	—	0	9	$\frac{9}{16}$
5 ditto —	ditto —	0	11	$\frac{61}{64}$
6 ditto —	ditto —	1	2	$\frac{11}{32}$
7 ditto —	ditto —	1	4	$\frac{47}{64}$
8 ditto —	ditto —	1	7	$\frac{1}{8}$
9 ditto —	ditto —	1	9	$\frac{33}{64}$
10 ditto, an Escudo,	—	1	11	$\frac{58}{64}$
11 ditto —	ditto —	2	2	$\frac{19}{64}$
11 $\frac{1}{14}$ ditto, a Ducado, ditto	—	2	2	$\frac{47}{128}$
12 ditto —	ditto —	2	4	$\frac{11}{16}$

13 Reals

APPENDIX.

	£.	s.	d.
13 Reals Vellon equal to	0	2	$7\frac{5}{64}$
14 ditto — ditto —	0	2	$9\frac{15}{12}$
15 ditto — ditto —	0	2	$11\frac{55}{64}$
$15\frac{1}{17}$ ditto make a Peso, or current Dollar, equal to —	0	3	0
16 ditto — ditto —	0	3	$2\frac{1}{4}$
17 ditto — ditto —	0	3	$4\frac{41}{64}$
18 ditto — ditto —	0	3	$7\frac{1}{12}$
19 ditto — ditto —	0	3	$9\frac{27}{64}$
20 make a Peso Duro, or hard Dollar, ditto —	0	3	$11\frac{58}{64}$
40 make an Escudo de Oro —	0	7	$11\frac{5}{8}$
60 make a current Pistole —	0	11	$11\frac{7}{16}$
75 make a gold Pistole —	0	15	0
100 ditto — ditto —	0	19	$11\frac{1}{16}$
320 make the Uncia de Oro	3	3	9
1,000 ditto — ditto	9	19	$2\frac{5}{7}$

Ecclesiastical revenues being reckoned by *Ducats*, I have subjoined the following table:

	s.	d.
1 Ducat is equal to —	2	$2\frac{47}{115}$
2 ditto — —	4	$4\frac{94}{}$
3 ditto — —	6	$7\frac{11}{}$
4 ditto — —	8	$9\frac{60}{}$
5 ditto — —	10	$11\frac{107}{}$

6 Ducats

APPENDIX.

	£.	s.	d.
6 Ducats are equal to —	0	13	2 $\frac{16}{}$
7 ditto	0	15	4 $\frac{73}{}$
8 ditto	0	17	6 $\frac{120}{}$
9 ditto	0	19	9 $\frac{19}{}$
10 ditto	1	1	11 $\frac{86}{}$
11 ditto	1	4	2 $\frac{5}{}$
12 ditto	1	6	4 $\frac{52}{}$
13 ditto	1	8	6 $\frac{99}{}$
14 ditto	1	10	9 $\frac{18}{}$
15 ditto	1	12	11 $\frac{65}{}$
16 ditto	1	15	1 $\frac{112}{}$
17 ditto	1	17	4 $\frac{11}{}$
18 ditto	1	19	6 $\frac{78}{}$
19 ditto	2	1	8 $\frac{125}{}$
20 ditto	2	3	11 $\frac{44}{}$
30 ditto	3	5	11 $\frac{2}{}$
50 ditto	5	9	10 $\frac{46}{}$
100 ditto	10	19	8 $\frac{21}{38}$
500 ditto	54	18	7 $\frac{12}{38}$
600 ditto	65	18	4 $\frac{5}{18}$
1,000 ditto	109	17	3 $\frac{3}{18}$
2,000 ditto	219	14	6 $\frac{3}{8}$
3,000 ditto	329	11	9 $\frac{9}{10}$
4,000 ditto	439	9	0 $\frac{3}{4}$
5,000 ditto	549	6	3 $\frac{13}{16}$
6,000 ditto	659	3	7 $\frac{1}{8}$
8,000 ditto	878	18	1 $\frac{1}{8}$
10,000			

APPENDIX.

	£.	s.	d.
10,000 Ducats are equal to	1,098	12	$7\frac{1}{2}$
16,000 ditto —	1,757	16	3
20,000 ditto —	2,197	5	$3\frac{1}{4}$
30,000 ditto —	3,295	17	$11\frac{5}{8}$
40,000 ditto —	4,394	10	$7\frac{1}{2}$
60,000 ditto —	6,591	15	$11\frac{1}{4}$
80,000 ditto —	8,789	1	3
100,000 ditto —	10,986	6	$6\frac{1}{4}$
150,000 ditto —	16,479	9	10
1,000,000 ditto —	109,863	5	$7\frac{1}{2}$
2,000,000 ditto —	219,726	11	3
4,000,000 ditto —	439,453	2	6
8,000,000 ditto —	878,906	5	0

INDEX.

INDEX

TO THE

THIRD VOLUME.

ACIDS, how formed by nature? 90
Agriculture of Alicant 196
——— ——— Carthagena 134
——— ——— Valencia 269
Alcala de Chivet 301
A'cerrazas - 32
A. nes, their ravages in Spain - - 219
Alhama - - 48
Alhambra, at Granada 61
Alicant - 168, *et seq.*
Almanza, battle of 228
Almafora - 298
Alpargates 118, 130

Alvatera - - 161
Amulets, used at Alicant 166
Antonio, San. Marquis, murdered by smugglers 46
Aqueduct of Almafora 296
Archbishop of Valencia, his character - 274
Arbitrio, a municipal tax 73
Army, *v.* Military.
Arroyo, de la Miel 35, 38
Asalto, Count, captain general of Catalonia 319
Assassinations, frequent in Spain - 144

Banditti,

INDEX.

Banditti, in Catalonia, repressed - 327
Baranco, a ravin 105
Barilla, its species 131. 176.
- - 195
Baths of Buzot - 200
Baza - - 105
Beatification of saints at Barcelona - 337
Beggars, encouraged at Malaga - - 17
———— Granada 57, 58
———— Alicant 183
———— Valencia 251. 252
Benicarlo - 302
Bishop of Barcelona, his character - 320
———— Gerona 321
Boucher's opiate 342
Brandy at Benicarlo 303
Bucarros - - 32
Burjasot, near Valencia 274
Buzot - - 200

Campo de Tarragona 310
Carthagena 121 et seq.
Card, contract for America 39
Castellon de la plana 296. 298
Catalonia, its population, taxes, and revenue - 322
Cavanes - 301
Chalk, at Picacente 271
Chalk and gypsum, their affinity - - 90

Chirivel - 110
Cinnabar, at Alicant 213.
233
———— near Valencia 271
Cicuta, its medical powers, and efficacy in Valencia 283
Commerce, bad principles of,
- - 259
Convicts, employed in public works - 125. 190
Contador - - 109
Corsarios, public carriers 96
Cortejos, at Carthagena 145
Coscoja, Quercus Coccif. 202
Crillon, duke, cap. gen. of Valencia - 272
Criminals, employed in public works - 125. 190
Cullar de Baza 106

Diego, father of Cadiz, a famous preacher 147
Diezma - 97
Diseases of Malaga 23
———— Carthagena 136
———— Alicant 214
Dress of peasants near Lorca
- - 118
———— in Murcia 161

Earthquakes, frequent near Alicant - 231
Elche - - 162
Elda - - 226

Emfiteutic,

INDEX.

Emfiteutic, contracts in Catalonia - 328 *et seq.*
Equivalent, in lieu of provincial rents - 170
Esparto rush manufactured 96. 129. 177
Evaporation, cooling liquids 32, 33

Fishery at Alicant 179
——— Carthagena 128
Flagellants, at Malaga 14
Flies, troublesome in Murcia - - 156
Fontillon wine - 200
Fossils, extraneous, Murcia - - 158
——— Buzot 201
——— Alicant 212. 214
——— Xativa 232
——— Tortosa 309
Fuente la Higuera 229
Funda, a Spanish hotel 306

Gardoqui Antonio, the inquisitor - - 82
Garrote, for strangling nobles - - 79
Gerundio, Fray, his work condemned - 146
Ginjolero fruit - 135
Gipsies, numerous in Spain 307, 308

Gipsies, edict respecting 308
Granada - 55, *et seq.*
Granakermes 179. 202
Granaries, of Nules, in limestone rock - 295
Grao, near Valencia 275
Guadix - 99. 101

Hills, their formation 100. 309
Hospitalet . 309

Ilici, *v.* Elche.
Influx to Mediterranean, accounted for - 2
Inquisitors, paid by confiscations - - 286
——— more moderate than formerly . 334

Knives, for assassination 103

Liquorice, growing wild 160
Locusts, the species found in Spain - 206
Lorca - - 115
Lunatics in Spain 343

Maestranza, of Valencia 276
Malaga - 10, *et seq.*
Mal de Ojos - 165
Manesita, an amulet 166
Martinis, D. Joseph, of Malaga - - 16
Masdevall,

INDEX.

Mafdevall, doctor, his opiate
      137. 341
Military regulations in Spain
 - - 186
Mines in Catalonia 344
Mining districts, subject to poverty - - 345
Mongat, near Barcelona 320
Monjus - 313. 314
Monks, Franciscan, their orders - - 13
Monte pio, at Malaga 39
——— at Valencia 253
Montesa, ruined by an earthquake - 231
Moors, their expulsion, 73 to 78
Morviedro - 292
Mulberries, their species in Spain - - 264
Municipal government, corrupt in Spain 143
Murcia, its vale 150
——— the city 152

Nitre, v. Saltpetre.
Nobles, formerly oppressive in Valencia - 287
Nules - - 294

Opiate of Doctor Mafdevall
 - - 137
Opositor, and opposition, the terms explained 247

Orihuela - - 159
Oropesa - - 299
Oxen used for draught 54. 133

Pacheco, D. Fr. governor of Alicant - 183
Palm-trees, their variety 162
Palmitos, at Carthagena 136
Pantano, at Alicant 191
Papin's air machine 32
Parillena - 99
Penilla - - 118
Peon Caminero 167. 231
Perello - 309
Personero, del Comun, 20
Physicians in Spain, disciples of Piquer - 281
——— poor, and little respected 282. 340
Plantations, royal edict for, 261
Playhouse, near Valencia 276
Ploughs in Spain 53. 268.
        309
Poor, v. Beggars, Workhouses.
Population of Catalonia 322
——— principles of 107
Pot ash, v. Barilla.
Preachers, not excellent in Spain - 145
Presidiarios, or galley slaves
       122. 124.
Provisions, the price of, 41.
         50.

INDEX.

50. 95. 97. 111. 119. 148. 158. 163. 289. 313.
Pudding stone - 49
Putrid fever, at Malaga 23
Puzol, near Valencia 291

Quemadero, for burning heretics - - - 83
Quercus Coccifera - 202

Refresco, a Spanish entertainment - - 278
Revenue of Catalonia 326
Ribalta, a native of Castellon - - 297
Roblar - - 231

Sætabis - - 232
Saffron, collected at Albazete - - 179
Saguntum - 293
Salt-petre, how formed by nature - 87 to 92
San Felipe - - 232
Sax - - - 226
Sea breeze, theory of, 5
Sierra Nevada - 55
Silk worms, their natural history 265, et seq.
Silk, its introduction and progress in Europe 267
Silk winding, at Alicant 195

Silk manufacture at Valencia - - - 254
Silk, trade between England and Spain 257. 263
Shingle, smooth gravel 49. 150
Smugglers, on the mountains in Spain 47. 52. 60
Solano, Don Felix, his plantations - - 35
Superstition of the vulgar respecting the patronage of saints - 215

Tarragona - - 311
Tartil, a tax - - 73
Taxes of Catalonia 324
Tenure in Catalonia 332
Torreblanca - - 301
Torres de la Costa, a tax 73
Tortosa - - 305
Tuf, a calcarious incrustation - - 38
Turners, at Alicant 178

Valencia - 235, et seq.
—— its climate favourable to invalids - 284
Vegetation, rapid in the south of Spain - 199
Velez el Rubio 110
Velez Malaga - 44
Venicafe

INDEX.

Venicafe las Cafas de	299	Weights and meafures	134. 223. 288
Venta, a folitary inn	104	Wheat, the commerce of, regulated	259
Venta de Jimenao	149		
Vertientes	108, 109		
Villa Franca de Penades	316	Wines, their kinds and price	29. 292. 302, 303
Villa Real	296		
Villa Vieja	294	Workhoufes	69. 184. 251
Villena	226		
Vineyards, their expence	28	Xativa	238
Uldecona	304	Xixena	112

F I N I S.

Published by the Author of this Journey,

And frequently referred to in the present Work,

A DISSERTATION on the POOR LAWS;

AND

OBSERVATIONS on VARIOUS PLANS OFFERED FOR THE RELIEF of the POOR.

Lately published, by C. Dilly,

FREE THOUGHTS on DESPOTIC and FREE GOVERNMENTS, as connected with the Happiness of the Governor and Governed. Crown Octavo.

Direction to the Binder.

The three Plates of Implements of Husbandry are to be placed at the end of the Third Volume.

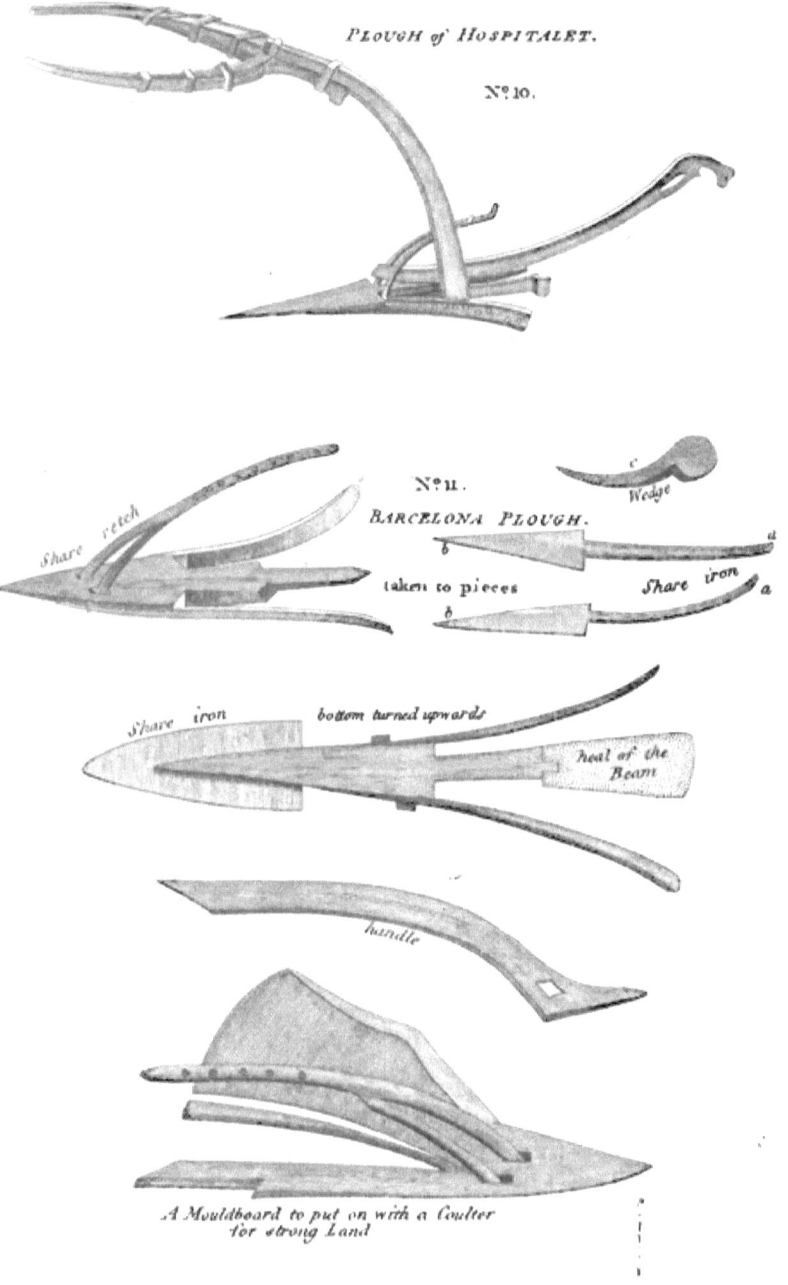

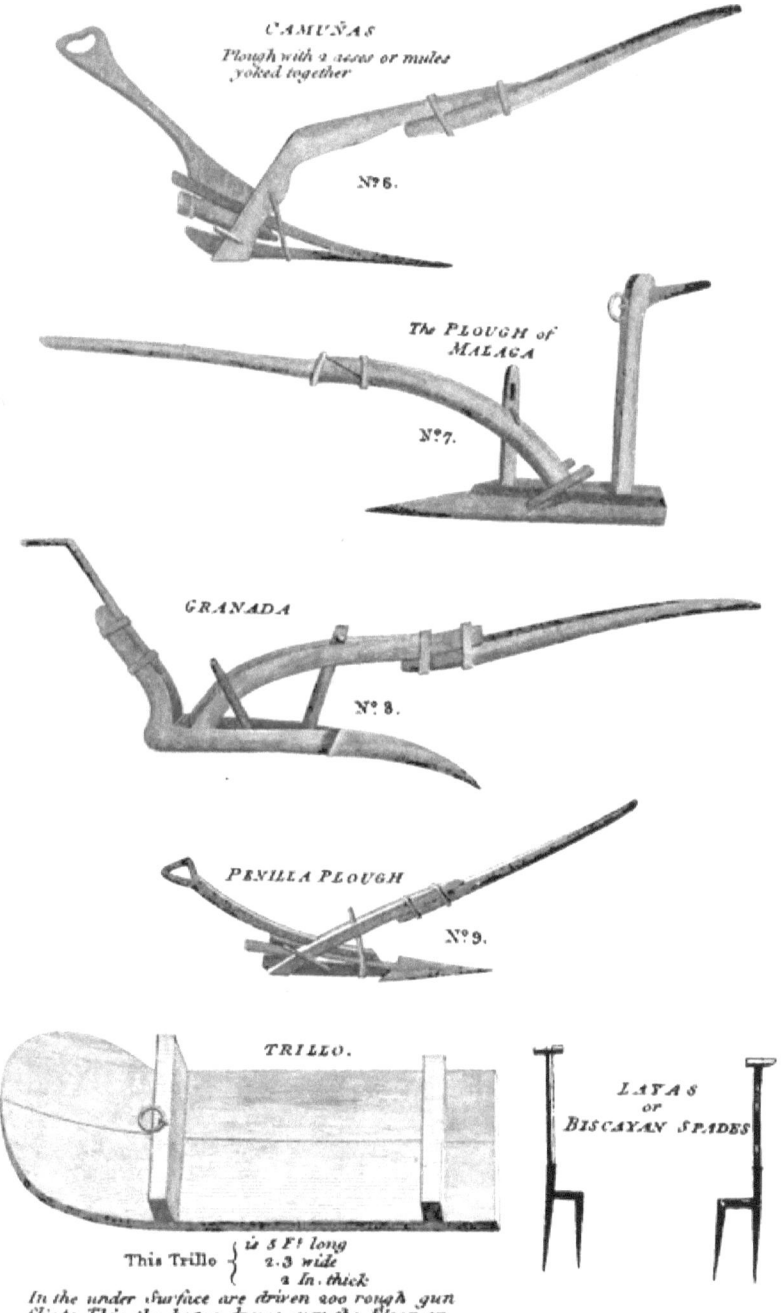

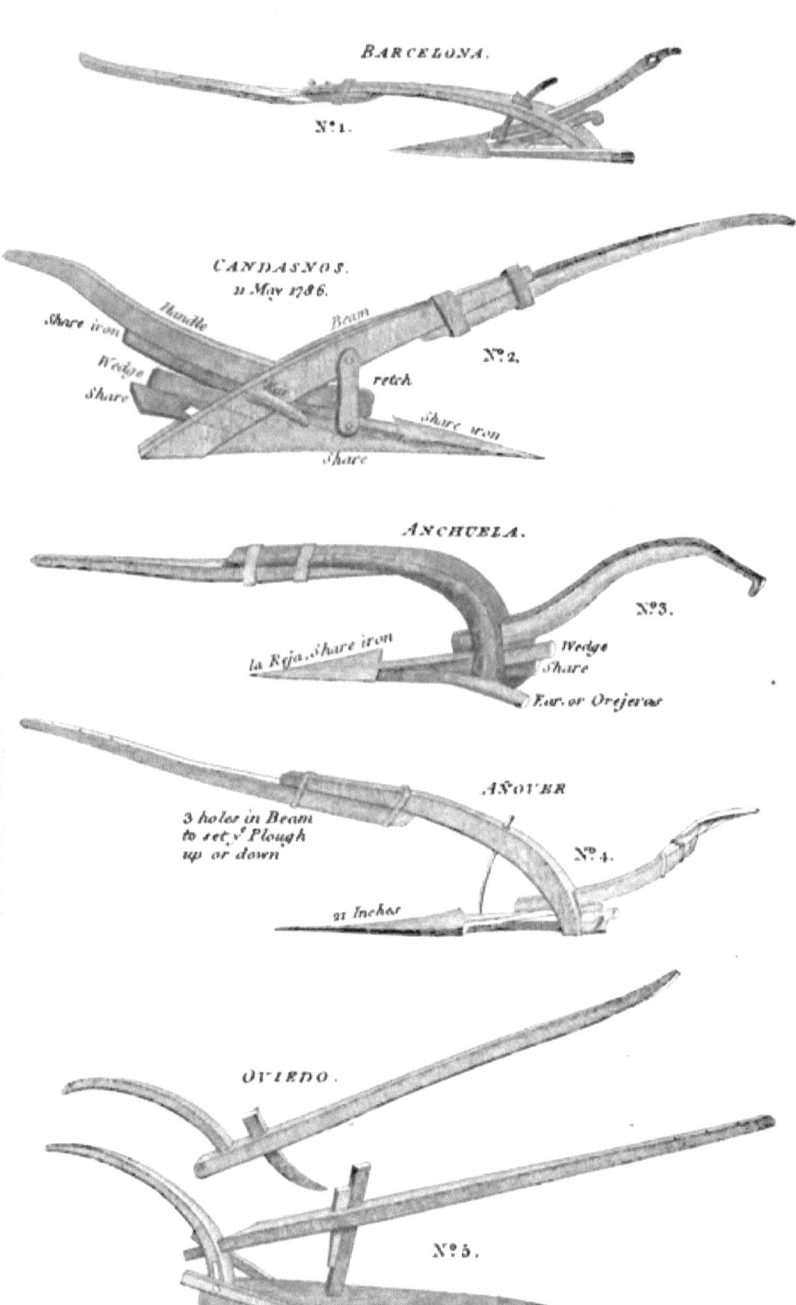